Key to Personal Freedom
How Myths Affect Our Family Lives

By Susie Walton

Practical Tips for Every Day Parenting

Published at:

PO Box 167

Cardiff, CA 92007

www.indigovillage.com

ISBN 978-0-578-00719-9

Introduction

I feel this is an extremely timely book because of the urgent need to crack so many outdated and unproductive myths about parenting. These myths are deeply seated beliefs that influence the way we view a situation and how we respond to it. These beliefs usually stem from the way we were raised as children and what we have heard or seen over the years.

If we look at the high incidence of child and teen behavioral problems, law infractions, and even suicide, it becomes obvious that many of the old beliefs are not working. Parents want the best for their child, but may not have the necessary tools to raise resilient, responsible, capable, and emotionally stable children. I have been teaching and implementing these skills, for the past twenty three years. These classes have amazed parents and caregivers with their effectiveness and simplicity.

Children are constantly gathering information through nature, teachers, prayers, intuition, family and friends. They are curious. Have you noticed how often children ask the question "Why?" or "How come?" They love to learn.

I invite each of you to become more curious. Begin asking questions, gathering information and resources. The more information you gather, the more choices you have. This will empower your decisions for your family, team, or classroom. This is what I intend to give you through my book: the chance to become your own best expert when raising your children, to be all they can be, and for you to have a healthy and resilient relationship with each child. Your children love you. They want to feel connected to you. These ideas will support this connection.

Both my students and my four sons encouraged me to write this book. *Key to Personal Freedom: How Myths Affect Our Family Lives* is the result of their requests. It is full of entertaining and insightful stories from parents and caregivers who have taken my classes. I use these stories to illustrate new views on old myths. At the end of each chapter, I give practical and easy tips that you can implement instantly in your home or classroom.

I added stories written by and about my four sons, who have been my teachers and my friends during my parenting years. Stories are easier to remember than facts. They are also more fun. So enjoy this book and enjoy the wonderful journey of raising great kids. If you listen, feel, and put these ideas into practice, you will create a strong, resilient, and loving family.

Love and Blessings, Susie Walton
San Diego, California 2009

Acknowledgements

First and foremost I am in such gratitude to my sister, Ramloti, who, with her unconditional love and guidance supported me in turning my dream into a reality.

Special thanks to Karen Bassett, Pam Dunn, Ana Ubensmith, Kailash, David Ryan, Cindy Cleary, Nancy Rapp, Cindy Silbert, Kathryn Kvols, Robert Evans Studios, my family, friends, and graduates for your stories and support. It truly does take a village to write a book.

Most importantly, much gratitude and love to my sons Adam, Nathan, Luke and Christopher. You are truly the wind beneath my wings.

Forward

Key to Personal Freedom: How Myths Affect Our Family Lives is an important book to read and experience. If you want to be empowered and inspired as a parent, you will want to continue reading and then recommend it to every parent you know.

There was only one thing we knew for sure when our children were born – that was – that we loved them beyond description. Our hearts opened at the births of these beloved children. That heart opening expanded throughout many stages of their progression of their lives. While I experienced this with my own three sons, I also had similar feelings for nieces, nephews, cousins and my friends' children.

I just knew that this love would be all I needed to parent my children! I soon realized that was not true. That came about when my son was acting out of character (meaning he was having a tantrum because I wouldn't let him have something I thought he shouldn't have)! I didn't know what to do, so I forgot about how much I loved and adored him and then yelled at him. When he finally calmed down and gave me MY way, I realized I did not feel good about the way I handled that situation. Although I could justify my actions, it did not alleviate the feelings I had. I don't believe my son or I were empowered.

The philosophy of this book will empower you during the many challenges of raising children. One of those challenges is to debunk the myths of parenting long held within our society. Susie Walton empowers you to follow your heart and your intuition (your magnificence) while providing real life examples. These examples are empowering and inspiring. The stories touched and opened my heart, while the tips gave me the concrete description of how to parent in an inspiring way, bringing out the magnificence of my love and allowing my children's light to shine ever so bright!

So immerse yourself in this book. *Key to Personal Freedom: How Myths Affect Our Family Lives* will open your heart, expand your mind and renew your faith in yourself.

Pamela P. Dunn
Your Infinite Life Training and Coaching Company
Author of *It's Time To Look Inside*

Table of Myths and New Ideas

Dedicated to all families; as we are all
part of the 'village of humanity'.

Myth One:
Discipline Creates Distance.

This myth is old, but true if you were raised in an autocratic household. In this type of household, the parent was the boss and if you did not obey you were punished. By the time you were a teen many of us were not connected to our parents and we certainly did not share information with them about what was going on in our life! Do you know that the majority of teens want to go to their parents when they have a problem or concern? Most of them do not go to their parents in fear of being lectured, grounded, yelled at or knowing their parent will not sleep for the next three months if they do, so it is not worth going to them!

New Idea:
You can Discipline and Stay Close with Your Kids and Make a Great Family Team

So, how do we discipline and stay connected? In that moment when you want to yell or you are so frustrated that you feel like spanking or putting kids in 'time out', pause a moment. In that moment, take some deep breaths, or walk away for a few seconds to self-calm. Then ask yourself the question, "Do I want to create distance or closeness right now?"

Teaching Point:

We distance ourselves from our children when we yell, threaten, shame, or blame them. An example is when we yell with an angry or frustrated tone, "How many times have I told you not to spill your milk!" That may take care of the problem, but they will feel disconnected from you.

There are healthier ways of disciplining than yelling or spanking, which is what we often do when we are frustrated. The pause is important because it allows us to respond to the situation instead of just reacting. In that pause some options are: take a deep breath, count to 10, take a sip of water, or maybe just get eye level with your child. Do what works best for you.

In that moment, think to yourself, "I can discipline and stay connected." Instead of saying, "How many times have I told you not to spill your milk," you might say, "Lets figure out a different way for you to pour your milk and keep it from spilling." Or, "Okay, so you spilled the milk, what needs to be done to get it cleaned up?"

Story: Chocolate Floor

My three-year-old son and I were in the kitchen and he dropped a half-full container of Chocolate Nesquik mix on the kitchen floor. As taught in my parenting class by Susie, instead of yelling at my child and creating distance, I paused

---

a moment and took a deep breath. I then looked at him and said, "What do you need to do with that?" He proceeded to get the scooper and scooped the chocolate mix off the floor. Then I handed him a spray bottle of water and he sprayed the floor with water and scrubbed it. It was pretty cool.

Story: It's a Brand New Start to the Day

Before taking the class, just getting out of the house in the morning with both boys dressed, fed, teeth-brushed, shoes on, and in the car was too much. It was feeling like a war zone rather than a family.

The change I like best is the spiritual connectedness I feel with my children. When I think differently, get out of my old pattern of doing things, and get on my children's level, I connect with them and we both win. I have found the more responsibilities that I give my two boys the less work and more harmony there is at home.

I am constantly surprised by how much my children want to help and how much they want to do. When I let them help around the house we all feel better. I like the principle of giving my children choices with consequences because it prepares them for what the future will bring and it makes them less dependent on me. It has definitely softened the edges off our mornings and day–to-day stressful tasks. I am so grateful to have learned how to discipline and still stay connected and close to my children.

Story: Spelling Quiz

My son Grant is in third grade. The school year has been in session for eight weeks and he is starting to get the hang of his new responsibilities. His teacher explained, "Third graders have to become even more responsible than ever before and must be accountable for their actions." As a mom, I want to support this effort to help him learn and grow.

Two weeks ago we were discussing homework while driving in the car. We were practicing spelling words out loud to get ready for a test the next day and Grant was feeling anxious. I was trying to help Grant see that practicing out loud is a tool to help learn the words, you don't have to see them first. As part of the conversation, I said, "How well do you think you would do if one day you were given a test on a list of spelling words that you hadn't seen before?" Grant said, "I would get a zero." I could see that his confidence level was not very high.

Interestingly, yesterday, that very thing happened! It was Monday and Grant had a spelling test, and while eating breakfast, he realized he hadn't studied his spelling words at all and he began to panic, freak out, cry, and blame me. He looked at me with angry, tear-filled eyes and I felt terrible, but I knew he had to learn from this. I knew the natural consequence of forgetting to study would teach him the very lesson he needed to learn and I told him he would have to bear the consequences.

Unfortunately, he felt he was going to FAIL MISERABLY. Just then, my daughter Marisa, seven-years-old, reminded me of the conversation in the car. So I said, "Hey Grant, remember when we talked about taking a test without having seen the words?" He looked at me with curiosity. "What do you think about experimenting with this test to see what you can do?" His eyes lit up, he liked the idea.

He went to school and came home with a 100% on the test and 100% confidence. I ended up receiving a big hug and a very sincere, heartfelt "Thank you Mom." The moral of the story: I held Grant accountable for his actions even though it was hard to watch him struggle and it brought us closer together at the same time. We were both winners (and now my influence factor has likely increased in Grant's eyes).

Story: Cleaning Up

Katie and her friend Brittany were at my house and they said, "We're going to go outside and do something." I looked in the living room and saw all their trash from lunch sitting there so I said, "Well, how about starting here?" They looked, saw what they had left, picked it up and put it in the trash. This is an example of disciplining and staying connected.

The alternative was, "Come on Katie, how many times do I have to tell you, clean up after yourself!" In that manner, I'm getting the job done, but I'm creating distance between us. This is an example of the difference between the two ways of disciplining.

Story: Press Your Pause Button Dad

Once we had taken the parenting course, my husband began touching his forehead as symbolically as his 'Pause' button. My, 3 at the time daughter apparently noticed this motion and on one occasion, my husband was beginning to get upset about something and she very gently walked over, stared for a few moments at his forehead and then slowly pressed her two fingers into the center of his forehead. It was clear she wasn't exactly sure what she was pressing, but that something on his forehead magically worked. It did on that day because he just burst into laughter. As she has gotten older she now just says "Press Your Pause Button" and we say it to her as well. It's very effective all the way around!

Story: Stupid Mommy

My five-year-old daughter, Madison, became upset with me one evening because I wouldn't allow her to open the mail until she put her toy Jeep away. She became extremely frustrated with me and started calling me "stupid mommy" and pretended to hit me. She moved so quickly from the goal of power to the goal of revenge that my head was spinning. I had to walk away (pause) to take a breath before responding, which only infuriated her more.

Once I calmed myself, I walked back into the room, knelt down next to her and said "you can call me all the names you'd like, but it won't change how much I love you." I gently guided her over to her artwork area, handed her markers and paper and walked away without saying a word.

Five minutes later she walked into the kitchen and handed me a drawing, then returned to her artwork without saying a word. The drawing was a picture of me with a funny face and the words "stupid mommy" at the top. As I read it, I couldn't help but be amazed at how clever she was to be able to express herself through her art.

Five minutes later, when she handed me her next drawing, I welled up with tears. It was another picture of me smiling, with the words "nice mommy" at the top. I could see this as re-enforcement of how important it is for me to come from my heart when being with my children and not reacting to their words or actions.

Teaching Point:

For younger kids, getting into their world and asking them what's important to them is very valuable. If you are having trouble about a certain issue, first take a pause, then ask the child with curiosity, not judgment, why they are behaving a certain way.

Story: Fireman Clothes

I used to get really mad at my son because every night he was supposed to get his clothes ready for school the next day. He would always make a big wad of his clothes in the middle of his room. I was getting rather frustrated with him. One time I took the time to ask in a calm tone, "Why do you always bundle your clothes in the middle of the room? They get all wrinkled for the next morning for school." My son said, "Well that's how the firemen do it." He had been to a firehouse and had seen how they put their clothes and boots in a pile so if there is a fire they don't have to go looking for anything. It made me understand so much more what was going on from my child's point of view.

Teaching Point:

Take some time with your teens or pre-teens and have them write down some of the activities they enjoy doing. Write down some of the activities you enjoy doing and see what you have in common. Those are the things you can do together.

When my sons were teenagers, there were three things they loved to do: eat, go to the beach, and go to movies. I could pretty much be assured they would spend some time with me if I told them I would take them to dinner, to the beach or to a movie. So those are the kind of things you can do to create closeness and stay connected.

Trust me, you are not going to have a lot of things in common, and you aren't supposed to. It is the job of a teen to start breaking away from a parent and figuring out what is best for him or her. But through it all, if there has been a sense of team and closeness in the family, the impressions and lessons learned together will stay with your kids for the rest of their lives. Here are some impressions of family from my four sons.

<u>Walton Story by Adam</u>

When I think of family, what comes to mind first are my brothers, mom, and dad. As a young child, our days were spent playing, laughing, and fighting. I remember hiking the canyons behind our house with my brothers and my mom. As we got older, we would go in the canyon by ourselves and make forts. With three brothers and a lot of other kids in the neighborhood, there really was no need to worry about having friends over. I did not even spend much time at preschool because I loved being at home.

My brother, Nate, and I loved wrestling. Usually one of us would end up crying but we would always do it again. We moved a lot as kids because of my dad's work, but it wasn't too bad since I always had my brothers, my mom, and my dad to hang out with.

As we got older, we started making a lot of friends, especially through basketball. We had some amazing games of basketball in our backyard. A neat thing about my family, especially my brothers, is that we all shared our friends. We grew up in an environment where we always had people living with us or visiting us, not to mention that we had 44 cousins. So we grew up being comfortable with people. I think that is why our friends are always so comfortable coming over and hanging out.

Walton Story by Nate

Our parents taught us that family is the most important thing in our lives. They are our teachers, our partners, and we are all here to help each other. In our family, each of us plays different roles at different times for each other. We all know that if any one of us needs any one else, we will always be there for them. In particular, I can remember times when things had not been going well or I'd been upset and angry. In those moments, I knew I could call my brothers or my mom. My mom reminds me to calm down and relax and think about the big picture. She helps me to realize that what is going on is just part of life and that it will all be okay. Somehow, I always feel better about it at the end of the call.

I think a lot of the bonding in our family occurs doing the little things. People make a big deal about the big things but life is made up of the little things. In our family the little things were the long hours at board games, the car rides together, the camping trips, the dinner table, driving to school in the morning, and telling each other, "I love you."

One of the things our mom taught us at a young age was to always tell each other "I love you" every time we said goodbye. When she was young, her dad passed away and she did not get the chance to say she loved him. She always said she regretted not telling him and so she always told us every time when she said goodbye that she loved us and we do that with each other. Sometimes people laugh at us because my brothers and I call each other on the phone, sometimes every day, and say "I love you" when we say goodbye. It is just one of the things our family does and we just want to reaffirm our commitment to each other.

Walton Story by Luke

I love being part of my family. There is nothing more important to me than my family and I think my whole family feels the same. I hope that when I get married I have a very close family as well and I plan to keep them in close contact with my brothers and parents. I will try to raise them like my mom raised us with open communication and sharing in the home and lots of love. We did a lot of family trips as kids.

Looking back, one of my favorite times was in the summer. As soon as the summer would start, every morning, my dad and mom would load up the big white pickup truck with all of us and our friends, along with coolers full of food and drinks. We'd get to the beach by 8:30 in the morning and we would stay sometimes until the sun went down. Whether we were playing football on the beach or volleyball, or just running around doing stupid things that kids do, we would do it pretty much all day, all summer long. Whenever we had friends sleep over they would come with us to the beach the next day. That was always one of my favorite times as a kid.

I talk to my brothers all the time and during the summer we always hang. I have a few friends that I consider 'brothers' that are really close to me, but my blood brothers are truly my very best friends. My strength, my success and my being is my family. Nothing is as powerful as the family bond.

Walton Story by Christopher

As I am sure everyone knows, my brother Luke is on the Los Angeles Lakers. Being that he is constantly in the media and the eyes of the public, he has had many opportunities to make public appearances for which he is paid by private companies for his efforts. Luke has always been an introvert and does not like to put himself in uncomfortable situations. Therefore, it seems to me that there must be considerable renumerations offered to Luke for him to agree to make an appearance for a company.

Recently Luke was asked to sign autographs at a convention for music companies. The company offered Luke a musical instrument of his choice as payment for his services. Luke has always been a lover of music, but has never had the urge to learn how to play an instrument. However, in the past few years I have taken up playing the guitar as a hobby. Luke was faced with a decision. He had to decide whether or not he wanted to make the appearance even though there was no benefit for him directly. He knows how much I enjoy playing the guitar and thought it would be a nice gesture for me to have a new guitar. Luke decided to do the appearance and he gave me the guitar. This selfless act by Luke displayed his love and support for his family members. He went out of his way to do something that in no way benefited his own life. He did it merely so I could enjoy a new guitar. This is just one of the many times my family has been there to provide support for me.

I remember when the Lakers were in the playoffs for the championship against Detroit. They had three games in a row out there and I knew it would be a rough time for Luke. I flew out to Detroit to be with him at the hotel and support him. Even though they lost the championship, I was glad that I was able to be there with him. I really appreciate my family and having been raised in such a loving atmosphere. No matter what happens in life, I seem to always have a family member there to support me or talk to me on the phone. And I try to do the same for my brothers. We really are like a team.

TIPS:

1. Seek to understand before being understood, (be curious.)
2. Remember to pause so you can respond instead of react.
3. When pausing: breathe, count to ten, or step away for a moment.
4. Ask kids questions rather than telling them what to do.
5. Use mistakes as an opportunity to teach.
6. Have fun.
7. Breathe.

Myth Two:
Children Aren't Old Enough
to Make Good Decisions.

Oftentimes, we as parents do not feel that kids are capable of making good decisions. We end up telling them what to do, how to do it, and when to do it! Essentially, we are raising robots who do not learn to think for themselves, we are not encouraging them to develop their critical thinking skills. How can we hope they will make good decisions when they are older if we do not allow them to make both good and not so good ones when they are younger.

New Idea:
Give them Choices.

So often we get stuck in a power struggle with our children. I can tell you right now that most kids (just like many adults) do not like to be told what to do. Here are some stories about giving choices to minimize power struggles.

Teaching Point:
There are different kinds of choices:
Concrete choices:

> *Would you like to set the table or clear the table?*

Playful choices:

> *Would you like to hop to bed or have a piggy-back ride to bed?*

Choices with incentives:

> *Would you like to finish your show and have one book or go to bed now and have three books?*

Choices with consequences, best with young kids;

> *Your choice is to hold on to the shopping cart or be put back into the shopping cart.*

When offering any choice add the phrase,

> *"It is your decision," it helps children learn that life is based on the decisions they make.*

Story: The Dentist Every Parent Wished For

I have been seeing this young patient for about one and a half years. He is almost seven years old. The first few times I was barely able to look in his mouth, even to do a simple exam. He was very squirmy and was constantly moving his arms and head. He would get very nervous when I would look in his mouth, closing it in a protective and nervous manner.

I had just attended a parenting class with Susie. This young boy was my first patient the next morning. From the first moment I saw him I started practicing my techniques. We talked about why he thought it was important to go to the dentist and the different things a dentist does. I thanked him for being on time to the appointment and asked him what would make it a nice appointment for him. Once he sat in the dentist chair we talked about the different things that he could do to help during his visit. I asked him if he wanted to have a quick visit or a long visit. He said a quick visit. I told him I felt he made a good choice. We talked about the different things he could help me with to make it a quick visit. We decided that keeping his hands to his side and his head still were good ways to help. I gave him the choice to either keep his hands to the side, on his lap, or on the arm rests. He recommended different ways to position his head. He made the choice to keep his head very still and with his chin slightly elevated.

After each decision, he was very happy with himself and became more and more excited to start implementing the decisions he made. During the course of the appointment, he kept asking me if he was being a good helper. Each time, I told him that he made a good decision and that he was sticking to his promises. The patient was very happy and seemed to be encouraging himself.

In our office, we have traditionally given prizes to children after the appointment. This is in conflict with the notion of not giving praise or rewards, however, it is an expectation in a dental office. After the appointment, the young boy asked me if he could get a prize. I asked him if he felt he deserved one. Very enthusiastically, he said yes. I asked him why and he told me because he was a good helper. I asked him what he did to help and he said that he followed directions and kept his hands and head where he had decided they would be at the beginning of our appointment. I told the young boy that if he felt he wanted or really needed a prize that he was welcome to take one. The difference between this visit and past visits was remarkable. The appointment went very smoothly with very few interruptions. The boy showed a great sense of accomplishment and an increase in self-confidence. He left with a big smile on his face instead of one of frustration and low-morale.

<u>Story: The Beauty of Choices</u>

We give our 21-month-old choices all the time so he feels like he has some control over his daily life and activities. In the morning I have him choose between two different shirts and he points right away to the one he wants to wear. When I put it on him he looks down at it with pride. At night we do the same thing with his pajamas. Who knew a 21-month-old could be so decisive!

When we go to the grocery store I do the same thing, I hold up two items and let him choose. When he brushes his teeth he chooses from two different kinds of toothpaste. Before I started doing that with him he wouldn't even brush his teeth. When we go down the driveway on his little scooter, he chooses one of two directions he can go. He knows not to go straight into the road but goes left or right because we have given him the right to choose.

Walton Story by Susie

When my youngest son was about 12-years-old, I asked him to take out the trash one evening. He said he did not want to so I said I would take out the trash and he could unload the dishwasher instead if he preferred. I said the decision was up to him. He decided to take out the trash.

Story: Life is Based on the Decisions we Make

It was getting close to bedtime and a dad told his two and a half year-old son: "It is your choice, if you want to finish watching the TV show, we'll have time for one book. If you want to turn off the television then we'll have time for three books, it's your decision." His son chose to finish the show. Dad put him to bed, read the one book and of course the son begged for one more. They had been giving choices lately so this was not new for the son. Dad said to his son, "you made the decision to finish the show and have one book. We'll try it again tomorrow." So his child cried for five minutes and after that he looked at his daddy and he said, "Daddy, I am so sad about my decision". So here we have a two and a half year-old child already figuring out what decisions are all about.

Teaching Point:

Can you imagine this child as a teenager? He is already learning that life is based on our decisions. Start using these words with your young kids now and if you have older kids, begin letting them make decisions. Remember to remind them they can always try it again later.

Story: Yeah Bud, That's how it Works

My six-year-old son Jordan and I are always talking about choices and consequences. On many occasions we have discussed the power he has to control what happens in his life based on the choices he makes throughout the day. One day after school I noticed that he was being exceptionally kind to his sister and me and that he was doing a really good job of pausing and calming himself down when he started to get frustrated or angry. I acknowledged this by saying to him, "Hey Bud, I really appreciate that you are being so kind today and that you are working so hard at pausing when you feel like you are going to get upset. It really helps things to run more smoothly in the house, so thank you." He said in return, " I understand now Mom, when you are kind to people they will be kind back to you and you will have a really good life." I said "Yeah Bud that's how it works."

Story: One Less Power Struggle

One mom who has four-year-old twins took the girls to stay with their grandmother for the weekend. When the girls came home she got a phone call from her mother-in-law. Grandma said that on Sunday morning while they were getting ready to go to church, one of the girls said that sometimes I have a choice and sometimes I don't. I want to make the choice not to wear tights today. Since it was not a cold day, her grandma agreed. Even at four kids can ask for what they want and make reasonable choices.

TIPS:

1. Have your kids start making decisions on negotiable events.
2. Give them two choices, and then say, "You make the decision." Be sure to stick with it even if they want to change the choice.
3. Be okay with them making a choice that doesn't seem to be the best one as there is no better way to learn than from our own mistakes.
4. Have fun!

Myth Three:
If you Give Kids an Inch,
They will Take a Mile.

Many parents I have worked with have a strong belief attached to this one. They believe if they do not make kids follow their commands, the kids will take advantage. As a result, the parents become even stricter hoping that the child will know who is boss, which often results in more power struggles and problems.

New Idea:
Kids Have Great Solutions
to Problems.

You will be amazed at the solutions your children can come up with. Take the time to ask for their help when you are in the middle of a power struggle or feel stuck on how to deal with a certain issue. The following stories provide insightful and easy ways to empower your children and make your job as a parent much more enjoyable! I cannot tell you how many times my kids have come to my rescue when I felt I did not have an answer or idea for solving a problem.

Walton Story by Susie
My teenage boys had a habit of leaving their dirty clothes and towels on the floor expecting me to pick them up and wash them. I told them that I was willing to do laundry, but

not willing to walk around the house and pick up their dirty laundry and wash it too. I asked them how we could make this work for all of us. They came up with the solution that I would continue to do the laundry as long as they put it in the laundry basket or in the laundry room. This worked for me.

Story: FAIR is FAIR

We learned never to assume that we knew what seemed FAIR to our children. The following is an example.

One lovely autumn afternoon near Halloween, my husband and our young son and daughter, ventured out to do some errands. Their last stop became the source of much excitement. They had gleefully purchased a huge, furry, battery-operated spider with which to terrorize their poor-unsuspecting mother. This premeditated joy came to a screeching halt however, during the car ride home. BOTH of our children wanted to HOLD the coveted spider. This seemingly small detail mushroomed into an enormous conflict, complete with a yelling, screaming tug-o-war while Tom was driving. Struggling to keep his eyes on the road and his sanity intact, my husband suddenly remembered that mantra: "Okay Guys, let's do a 'Win-Win' with that spider."

Now as a rational adult you may think, as Tom did, that this suggestion would likely lead to a "take-turns-holding-the-spider" approach. Not so, instead our children calmly negotiated what was for them, the perfect solution. Our daughter Lili held the spider the entire way home, while our gadget-loving son Kyle held the real prize, the BATTERIES! Now all parties were content and peaceful (including my husband), each secure in the knowledge that they had made the best deal. Everyone except me of course, because that wretched spider has startled me every Halloween since.

Story: Splish Splash She was Taking a Bath

One frustrated mom had a four-year-old who was always splashing water out of the bathtub. The mother would constantly say, "quit splashing" or "close the shower curtain" or "I'm going to punish you," and nothing would work. Finally she asked her four year old, "What can you do to keep the water in the bathtub?" The four year old turned to her mom and said, "I could close the shower curtain." Now this is something the mother had asked her to do a zillion times before, but because she finally asked the four-year-old, the child felt very powerful coming up with her idea. The shower curtain was closed and the problem was solved.

Teaching Point:

Because kids receive up to a thousand compliant statements a day, they eventually stop listening to what we are telling them to do. Whenever possible, remember to ask them what needs to be done or how a problem can be solved, rather then telling them what to do.

Story: Sometimes Kids Know Best

Children often have great ideas for solving a problem that may have never occurred to you as the parent. The following story is told by Kathryn Kvols, the co-founder of the parenting curriculum Redirecting Children's Behavior, and related on page 81 of her book by the same name.

I came home upset about a conflict I'd had with one of my employees. My five-year-old son, Tyler, could see that I was unhappy and asked me what was wrong. I told him about the situation and asked him if he had any suggestions about what I should do. He thought for a moment. Valentine's Day had just passed, and he suggested that I give my co-worker one of his Valentine cards. First I criticized the idea in my head, thinking how silly it would be to do that. Then I thought, "Why not?"

Tyler and I found a Valentine's card. I slipped it into an envelope and the next day I gave it to my employee, saying, "I felt so bad about what happened between us yesterday, Tyler suggested that I give you this Valentine." She started to cry, I started to cry, and we resolved the conflict right then and there. That night, I shared with Tyler what had happened and thanked him for helping me solve my problem. Imagine how proud of himself he felt for being able to help his grown-up mom solve one of her work problems!

Story: Cheeseburger in Paradise.

I was making cheeseburgers for dinner and had to use bread for the buns. While making dinner, my five- year-old decided he wanted a grilled cheese instead of a cheeseburger. I wanted him to have a burger, since I had a lot of meat that I did not want to go to waste. After a short negotiation, Thomas came up with the idea of having grilled cheese, with cut up hamburger on the side. We both thought it was a great idea, and he was thrilled. He ate his entire dinner (with a smile) AND helped with dishes! Yeah!

Story: Kefir to the Rescue

As Jade was getting a little older, she was entirely content to continue nursing, but I was ready for her to wean. It was becoming a distraction during our activities, but I did not want to force her to give it up. We talked about options with her and suggested she could replace the nursing with something special to drink.

One day at the store she saw kefir and announced that she wanted that to be her special drink. We took it home that day and she never nursed again. The special drink replaced nursing for a week or two and then she simply forgot about the kefir.

TIPS:

1. Ask your child or teen for help next time you feel stuck in a power struggle, whether it is with them or someone else.

2. Let your child, especially the first born, know you do not always have the answer or solution to the problem. Remember, you are new at this and you will make some mistakes, so be easy on yourself.

3. Use win-win techniques in which you both state how you are feeling and what you want. Then figure out a solution you both are okay with. This works great with teens.

4. Breathe.

5. Have Fun!

Myth Four:
Children Misbehave Because They are Spoiled or Bad.

This belief will put a lot of pressure on you as the parent because you will view the child's behavior as a reflection of you. As a result you will end up either threatening or punishing your child for their behavior, which may remove the symptom, but not deal with the real source of the behavior.

New Idea:
Children Misbehave Because Their Needs are Not Being Met.

We are the only species in the world that need more than food, water and shelter to survive. As a human being we need to feel a sense of importance, a sense of belonging, to feel love, and that we are valued. I feel parents of previous generations ago had an easier job with this principle. Most kids didn't go to school past age 14 because they were needed in the family business, whatever that may have been. If they were in school it was a one-room school with older kids helping out younger kids. During harvest time schools would close because the kids were needed out in the fields.

What about today? Where do our kids get that sense of importance and belonging? One of the reasons I feel gangs are so prevalent today is because kids want to belong. You see it when your six or seven-year-old first joins a team. The most important thing to them is the uniform! We love to belong.

Teaching Point:

The more discouraged kids become the more they will act out. It does not mean you should let them get away with their behavior. You will be more present and respectful handling misbehavior if you understand that it is your child communicating that one of his or her basic needs are not being fulfilled. These will show up as four different goals of behavior. These four goals are: attention, power, revenge, and avoidance.

Goal of Attention

Children with the goal of attention have a mistaken belief that the more time the parent spends with them, the more the parent loves them. With the goal of attention, you as the parent or adult will feel annoyed or irritated. This child can be both very charming and drive you crazy, as they equate love with keeping their parents with them. A key word to describe these types of children is engaging. Here is a story of how one dad handled the situation with his attention child.

Story: The Telephone Battle Turns Calm!

Every time dad would get on the phone, within minutes his child was coming up trying to get his attention. Normally, he would ask the person on the other line to wait a moment and he would spend the next fifteen seconds explaining to the child why he needed to wait. After about five of these interruptions, the caller finally told the dad that he would call back later. Dad was annoyed and irritated at his son and did not know what to do about it. It seemed no matter what explanation, bribe, or reward he offered, it never seemed to be quite enough.

The desperate father enrolled in the parenting course and learned how to redirect this mistaken goal of attention using the following four steps: Step 1: no eye contact. Step 2: no words. Step 3: take action immediately. Step 4: make the child feel loved. He went home and told his son what he would be doing now when the child wanted his attention during a phone call. He and his son actually role played it a couple of times.

The next time the phone rang and his son came up to him the dad simply gave no eye contact, used no words, took action immediately and made the child feel loved by rubbing his back as he continued talking on the phone. After he hung up the phone, the dad got down on eye level with his son, held his son's hands, and thanked him for waiting. Both the father and son felt good after the interaction instead of frustrated. The father was amazed at how successful and easy this was for him and his child.

Teaching Point:

A proactive approach for kids who love attention is creating a Genuine Encounter Moment (GEM) by Dorothy Briggs. Genuine encounters strengthen the relationship with your child. A GEM is simply getting down and looking at the child eye-to-eye when speaking to him and taking the time to listen to what he is saying. I have many parents who complain that their child never stops talking and asking questions. The parents never consider that they are rarely fully present for the child and so the child keeps asking for their attention. You will be amazed at what a difference it makes to get down on the child's level, make eye contact, and really listen to what they are saying. When children feel listened to, their need to continually ask for attention diminishes greatly. Another helpful tool is to touch the child as he is speaking with you. Touch is the road to a child's mind and you will find that your child will be able to focus a lot more on what you are saying to him.

Now we are all busy human beings and there may be moments when we cannot take the time to listen attentively to our child's story or questions. At that point, simply get down on his level and look him directly in the eyes and tell him you want to listen but need to finish your project first. Realistically, set a time when you would like to sit and listen to the child's story. This is still being respectful and it also shows respect for you. The important thing to remember is to keep your commitment to listening to the child. Often the child will get involved in something else and the temptation arises to leave him alone. I can assure you, however, that going to the child and telling him that you would like to listen now or answer his question will reap huge dividends in trust and the relationship you have with your child. If your child just plain loves to talk then get her a tape recorder and when you don't have the time to listen ask her to record the story so you can listen to it when you have the time.

Story: Snuggles by Pam

I was out of town on business. Drew was in second grade and I knew report cards would come home while I was away. I called the boys to ask them how they felt about their report cards. Bobby and Trevor had no concerns and they were inspired by their accomplishments. Drew got on the phone and I asked him about his report card. He stated that he received lots of "checks" (these represent "appropriate and acceptable" behavior). His voice then lowered and he let me know that he also had two "minuses" (as you may have guessed - this is for "unacceptable" behavior). As an aside - Drew is very social and loves to talk to everyone!

So, I asked him how he felt about his report card. He said that he felt good except for the "minuses." So I asked him what he wanted to do about that. He paused for about a minute and I could tell he was really thinking about the answer. He then, very proudly, stated, "I want to snuggle more!" As you can imagine, I had a HUGE smile on my face on the other end of the phone! I asked him, "So you think that if we snuggle more that will take care of the "minuses?" He said, "Yes!" I said, "You got it, we will snuggle more!"

With great pleasure, I followed through with this request making sure we snuggled more than what we had been and especially before and after I was away on business or they were at their Dad's. His next report card reflected no "minuses." I was in awe of the realization that he knew exactly what he wanted and needed when asked AND by the method he used to get my attention. What a brilliant child!

Story: Baby Blues

Most of the time when my 21-month-old son misbehaves it is because he is tired. When I push his nap time or bedtime he lashes out and hits me or hits other kids. When he is done eating and wants to get out of his high chair he starts throwing food. When I follow his signals and pay close attention to his needs he does not act out. Like all children he wants us to hear his needs. When I am present with him he is a happy, joyful kid. Before I get on the phone I spend quality time playing with him, reading or doing puzzles then I can get on the phone without him throwing a fit for my attention. If I walk in the door and haven't seen him for a while and I get right on the phone, well then he acts out...naturally.

Goal of Power

Power struggles happen to us in all walks of life. You will know you are in the middle of one with your child when you feel provoked or challenged or when you start thinking, "Who is the parent here?" When you find yourself in a power struggle, some options are: give choices; use one word; utilize conflict resolution or win-win; or acknowledge the power struggle to the child and ask for some help in resolving it.

The proactive approach for the child with the goal of power is to find ways to help your child feel that he is a valuable member of the family by asking his opinion or asking for his advice on the situation. Here are a couple examples of how to redirect when caught in a struggle or when you find yourself getting into one.

Story: Bedtime Struggle

One night when I told my son to go to bed he responded with, "I do not want to go to bed and you can not make me." I found myself entering into a power struggle as my tone of voice escalated. Noticing this, I sidestepped the power struggle and said to my son in a calm voice, "this is not working, what are we going to do." My four-year-old said, "you could stop yelling at me, dad." I said, "You are right, I should not be yelling at you, so what are we going to do?"

He said, "I could go to bed." I said, "That would be great," and off he went to bed.

Walton Story: Power struggle with Luke

When Luke was 16 I went to pick him up at his dad's house. I knew his older brother, Nate, was heading to the University of California at Santa Barbara for the weekend with some friends. When I arrived I found Luke in the car with his brother and friends. I asked him what he was doing and he said he was going to UCSB with them. I said "no you are not" and he said "why not?" I told him he was too young and did not need to be going there for the weekend. We were certainly getting into a power struggle and one I was feeling I would not win so I stopped for a moment and asked myself why I did not want him going.

After a bit of silence I said, "the reason I cannot let you go is that if I do I will not sleep for a moment until you are back because I will be so worried about you." Luke looked at me, got quiet, finally got out of the other car and got into mine and off we went. Now, he did not speak to me for an hour or so but soon everything was fine and I slept that weekend.

Teaching Point:

Often times we think we can just tell kids what to do, but if we actually unpeel the onion and get to the real reason behind our concern, we will have a much better chance of him or her being okay with it, especially teens.

Story: The Manager

Veronica started kindergarten last August and as of March, we still had a battle each morning to get to school on time. She is a free spirit, and is easily distracted by playing with her little brother or her toys rather than focusing on getting ready each morning. She is also notoriously slow at everything, such as eating breakfast. She gets into dividing up her fruit loops by color or seeing what animal shape her bagel looks like with each bite.

We tried numerous methods to address the problem including: using a timer for each task, saving up time from each task to use for "play time" before school, chore charts with pictures, giving choices, reducing the list of morning chores such as making the bed, star charts (didn't even work for the first day), discussions, lectures, having her go to the school office for tardy slips when late, sitting in the principal's office for recess when late, etc.

We finally sat down for another discussion one evening, and I asked her for any suggestions on how to improve our mornings so we could get to school on time because we were out of ideas. I expected a blank stare as before. She suggested that she be the "manager of the morning," and be in charge of telling us what we needed to be doing. She is a power child, and our power struggles have reduced significantly. One thing we have implemented was to give her little tasks to empower her, such as "manager of the parmesan cheese" when we are having spaghetti. She took this a step further, and put herself in charge of the mornings.

In the last three weeks since we began this, she has not been late to school, and our mornings are much easier. Instead of me nagging and pleading with her to get dressed, eat, brush teeth, etc., she tells me each step and what to do next. I find she is now saying the things I used to say if I don't respond to her fast enough- she'll say "Come on, we are supposed to be brushing teeth now, you're taking too long!" I have to fight the urge to nag her, and be careful not to fall into the old habit of telling her what to do. The mornings are much less stressful for me now that I have turned the control over to her, and she is responsible for the consequences of being late to school (recess in the principle's office). Best of all, our emotions are in check and our relationship is intact when I drop her off at school, so we are starting the day on a much better note.

Story: Boss of the Dinosaurs

I watched four three-year-olds in a playgroup. One little boy loved to say no. One day they were playing at a little table. He was playing with some dinosaurs and a little girl got up. He took her seat and when she came back he wouldn't move.

He made it very clear that there was nothing anyone could do to make him give up that seat. It seemed kind of silly to me, the other seat was open, but then I realized that he wanted more power. So I said to him, "it looked like you were having fun playing with those dinosaurs, how would you like to be in charge of those dinosaurs in this chair over here?" He was completely okay with that idea. The little girl could then sit down where she wanted and everyone was happy.

Goal of Revenge

Oftentimes when we are angry or hurt by someone we lash out at them as a form of self-protection. We call this revenge. You will know your child is in revenge when you feel angry or hurt and feel like hurting back. Children most likely to engage in revenge are children who have been punished or spanked, picked on by siblings or bullies, dethroned by a new baby, feel entitled or feel disconnected from their parents. What we need to do is: acknowledge their feelings; refrain from discipline in the moment, and if you are feeling very angry step away until you can handle the situation in a calmer way; teach them to do a makeup (repair the mistake) and re-establish the relationship. Here is a story about a mom who was able to do it a bit differently and with respect.

Story: Come See my Fort

My child wanted to show me the fort he had made in the back yard, but I was too busy, brushed him off and hastily told him he would have to wait. Out of anger and feeling hurt, he began crying and kicked his little brother while running out of the room. I felt outraged at my son's action and decided a good spanking was due. Knowing that would only make him angrier plus it would not be modeling a healthy way to express anger I took a moment to calm myself. In a firm and loving voice I said, "I can see that you are extremely angry right now and it is okay to be angry, it is just not okay to kick. I want you to take a break until you feel calmer and then we can talk about how to express your anger in ways that will not hurt yourself or others."

When my son felt calmer I asked him how he wanted to do a makeup to his younger brother who he had hurt. I also did a makeup to my son for not being more respectful to him when he asked to show me his fort. I honestly did not have the time to see it at the moment but I could have at least gotten on his level, made eye contact and lovingly told him that I would like to see it when I was done with my chore. I told him I would like to spend some time with him in the fort. My son then said that his make up to his little brother would be to invite him to play with us in the fort too. So instead of a cranky afternoon for all, it turned into a fun family time together with many valuable life lessons learned.

Teaching Point:

The purpose of a makeup is to make amends for being out of integrity. This is best learned by the parent modeling this for the child.

Goal of Avoidance

When a young child feels overwhelmed she often disengages. In older teens and adults it plays itself out as depression. You know you are dealing with avoidance when you feel pity for the child and want to rescue her. The proactive approach is to encourage her, show her how much she can do, monitor her self-talk, and teach her to break tasks down in to small doable steps.

Walton Story by Susie:
Why Did You Name Me with So Many Letters?

Christopher gave an example of the goal of inadequacy at a developmental stage. He came home in tears from school because his homework was to write in cursive his complete name ten times. His full name is Christopher William Walton and he wanted to know why I had given him a name with so many letters. For a young child, this was an overwhelmingly long name to write. So we worked on breaking down his name into smaller portions and in no time at all he had his homework finished.

Teaching Point:

This same experience can happen to a child with a homework paper full of math problems or a room full of toys. This can look to a child like it will take until the end of the world. Once again, asking the child what part of the math problems or toys he thinks he can handle in the moment is helpful. Then after a short break, he can complete the task.

Another tool for children who are feeling inadequate would be to find small successes for them to achieve. This will help them gain self confidence. For a child who gets overwhelmed picking up all the toys in his room, take a picture of the room when it is clean and put it on the wall. Then the child can look at it while he is cleaning to help him remember where things belong.

Story: Let's Go Shopping

A mom had a ten-year-old who displayed signs of inadequacy. So she took her to the shoe store to pick out a pair of shoes for her 18-month-old sister. Mom narrowed it down and had her daughter pick the one she thought was best. At first she said she couldn't, but mom said she could. Finally she picked a pair and they went home. They put them on the baby and everyone loved them. The ten-year-old's face just lit up!

Story: Doing too Much

In class, one of the most helpful ideas for me was to stop doing things for my kids that they could do for themselves. I always thought I was being helpful by getting them dressed and cleaning up after them all the time. Not only was I just making more work for myself, but more importantly, I was sending the message that I didn't think they were capable of doing it themselves. Not a great way to boost self-esteem!

At first, it was difficult. I heard a lot of whining and protests. I would simply say, "I know you can get your shoes on, I'll be back in a few minutes." I would leave the area and just let them have some time. Inevitably, I would come back and they would be standing by the door with their shoes on and big, proud smiles!

Or when someone would spill their milk, I used to rush to get a wipe. Now I just say, "Uh oh, your milk spilled. What are you going to do next?" I keep a large pile of wipes handy, and they are able to get one and wipe up their spill. It may not be as clean as I'd like it to be, but it's progress! In fact, my house hasn't been messier, but having the kids take part in "cleaning" and helping out really makes us a team and teaches them the importance of working together to maintain the house.

TIPS:

1. Give each child a Genuine Encounter Moment (GEM) a day.

2. Find ways to empower your kids. Many of the ideas already presented would help.

3. When your child is angry, validate his feelings even if you don't agree with him.

4. Teach him how to break down tasks into small doable steps.

5. Never give up on your children. It doesn't matter if they are two or twenty two! What they need to hear from you is that they will be okay for two reasons: Because you know who they are, and because they have you to support them.

6. Breathe and have fun!

Myth Five:
Children are Not Very Capable.

For different reasons we often do not think our kids are very capable and as a result we end up doing too many things for them. The more you do for your child the more you weaken your child. If we view our kids as not capable how will they be capable teens and adults? They will end up looking to others for guidance and not within, which is where the true answer lies.

New Idea:
Kids are Capable.
Be Willing to Ask for Their Advice.

Walton Story by Susie

Christopher is the youngest of my sons. When he was in fourth grade he loved rollerblading. One day I asked him to teach me how to rollerblade. He was very patient when teaching me and we had a blast. Later on, he asked his older brother Luke if he wanted to learn. Luke did, so outside they went. When they came back in the house you could see how happy Christopher was feeling having taught his mom and older brother how to rollerblade.

Teaching Point:

Kids love to be helpful if given the chance at a young age. Give children age-appropriate opportunities to help around the house. At early ages, children want to help with the dusting, the cooking, the table setting, and the cleaning. This is the easiest and best time to teach children these skills. It is helpful to the whole family and will be helpful to them when they move out and begin life on their own.

At first, it will take a little bit longer to show them how to dry the pan, how to fold the hand towel, how to put the napkins around the table, or how to dust the coffee table, but the dividends are well worth the investment.

Story: Kitchen Assistant

When my son Jacob was feeling left out because he had a new baby brother, he became my kitchen assistant. Here he was, two-and-a-half-years-old, and he's tearing up lettuce leaves and helping make a salad. The phone might ring and he'd hear me say, "I can't talk right now, I'm busy making dinner with Jacob and I'll call you back." This gave Jake a sense of power as an older brother helping out in the family. In a few years, Jacob became a big help with meal preparation and, eventually, he became chef at a five-star restaurant.

Story: Abracadabra

I tried just about everything to potty train Gavin (charts, stickers, toys, etc). He got the idea of going to the bathroom and did great most of the time, but he still had accidents.

He would be playing and would start doing 'the dance'. I would ask him "Do you need to go to the bathroom?" and every time, he would say "no." Inevitably, he would either have an accident a few minutes later or tell me he needed to go to the bathroom with only seconds to spare. When I would ask him why he didn't listen to his body, he would say that he was 'too excited and forgot.'

Susie suggested that I ask him if he was tired of having me ask, "Do you need to go potty?" He told me he was. We thought if he came up with his own word for needing to go to the bathroom, it might be better for him. Of course, he thought that was great and Abracadabra was born. Now, whenever Gavin needs to go to the bathroom, he says "Abracadabra" and off he goes to the bathroom. Ever since he created his word, he hasn't had an accident!

Story: Who Said You Had to be Two

My son Julien is not even two-years-old and I let him take glasses and plates out of the dishwasher. He loves putting them into the cabinet. It gives him a sense of purpose. He also loves taking clothes out of the washer and putting them into the dryer. He thinks it's a blast! Yes, I could get these things done a lot faster without him but it's much more fun to see the smile on his face when he helps me. I also put milk in a small cup and let him pour it on his cereal. He loves that! Who would have guessed someone so small is so capable?

Story: Empowerment 101

I found myself constantly solving problems for my kids. I thought it was my role as a parent. Susie helped me to realize that when I solved all their problems, it sent the message to them that I didn't think they could solve them on their own. One of my favorite strategies is to acknowledge their feeling of frustration or anger, and then say "I wonder what you'll do next?" Instead of fixing everything for them, I'm empowering them to figure things out on their own. Most of the time, they really just want acknowledgement of their feelings. ("Yeah, it's really frustrating when your Lego tower keeps falling! I wonder what you'll do next?") Once they know someone understands, it seems to open them up to finding solutions on their own. Instead of feeling helpless, they feel empowered.

Teaching Point:

Family councils are a great way to connect with everyone in the family at least once a week, particularly as your kids get older. Keep it short (15 to 20 minutes), keep it light and have fun. It is more important to have positive time together each week rather than solving every problem in the household.

Here is a format to follow:

Step One: Begin with an encouragement feast. (refer to page # 150).

Step Two: Discuss and problem-solve any issues that are taking place among the family members.

Step Three: Bring out a calendar and write down everyones' activities and appointments for the week. For younger kids, who are not yet reading, you can draw a picture or color code their activities.

Step Four: Have each person come up with a goal for the week and have the group come up with a family goal.

Step Five: Ask the kids how you are doing as parents.

Step Six: End in a fun way (play a game, have some popcorn, watch a movie together).

It is also a good time to give allowance. You can have a new leader each week and a secretary. A child three and older can be a leader. You might need to help him or her go through the agenda. The secretary will take notes.

If the secretary isn't writing yet they can draw during that time and then at the end of the meeting you can take the drawings and add some of the things you talked about at the meeting. I would date it and put it in a three ring binder and keep this as a memory. It's really a fun thing to go back and look at years later.

Story: Family Councils

At our family councils, the leader gets to choose a value for the week -- being kind, caring, patient, respectful, and sharing are just some of the values we discuss. We hang a small sign with the value over our kitchen table, next to our family mission statement, and sometimes talk over dinner about how we practiced that value during the day. We often ask, "how did we shine our lights in the world today?"

On two occasions recently, our five-year-old son, Marino, warmed our hearts by demonstrating our values. One morning as I was helping him get in his car seat, he picked a wild rose from our front garden, gave the rose a kiss, said he was "putting his love in and shining his light on it." He then handed it to me so I would have a good day. And one evening, we treated ourselves and had a pizza delivered for dinner. As I was fumbling for money to pay the pizza guy, Marino jumped up and said eagerly, "I'll pay the tip!" He ran to his piggy bank and came back with a couple dollars, just beaming that he could contribute to our family treat.

Story: Menu Planning Made Easy

At the end of our Sunday night family meetings, my husband and I along with our twelve-year-old twins plan the dinners for the week. We take turns selecting dinners for the week. Stress of menu planning is taken off of me, and I am no longer the boss. The kids learn how to make healthy choices, help with food preparations, and are excited when their chosen meal is served.

Story by Susie: When I was a Kid

When I was ten, my sisters and friends would work for what seemed like an eternity to put a carnival together with games and shows. We would then invite the neighbors to come to our yard to enjoy the carnival. We charged five cents and each of us earned 25 cents or so. Another time a bunch of us put a luncheon together at a friend's house, got dressed up, and invited our moms to attend, it was so much fun.

Another time, my friend and myself decided to put on a swim meet. We took all my medals, charged each kid 50 cents per event they entered and had a complete blast putting on the meet in Janie's pool. It was so amazing the freedom we had, our only guideline was to be home at six. We felt very capable and self reliant in our accomplishments with very little adult intervention.

Story: The Bike that Pedaled Itself

Taylor was not quite three and he hadn't yet mastered the tricycle. His tricycle had a pole attached to the back that I used to push him along, which made it completely unnecessary for him to learn how to pedal. One afternoon we set out around the block and this time I was not going to push. It took us about 30 minutes to go one block, but he was starting to get the hang of it. Every little seam in the sidewalk or incline of a driveway was a hurdle, but he kept going. After about 45 minutes he was pedaling steadily and said aloud "I am capable." I couldn't have said it better.

Walton Story by Susie

When my sister and I were first starting to teach we'd have my boys who were 9, 11, 13, and 15 help us as role players to get us used to teaching. Kids love to help out. When you are setting a goal and you need help, just ask for it. It makes them feel so important that their mom or dad needs their help. They are very capable! Just ask and you'll be amazed at the willingness and the cooperation, especially when it comes to meeting your goals.

Story: Jump Start

Our three year-old is very capable, but sometimes needs a little help in order to jump start a task. One of the best things he does for us is to take items from the kitchen over to the recycling bin or the trash. When we started him on these projects, he would do it willingly. The trash usually made it in the right spot.

Lately it has taken more of an effort to get him started. We asked him what would help him be more interested. The first idea was to have him either skip, jump or run to take the item over where it needs to go. That works well when he is in the mood to be playful. The second idea is to sing "Wheels on the Bus" loudly. We sing another verse when he returns. That usually perks him right up and he participates willingly.

Story: Pizza Bed

I was having trouble getting my kids to make their beds. When I asked for their advice they came up with this solution. My kids love this one. We pretend the bed is a giant pizza and we are going to make it. The fitted sheet is the dough and we smooth it out. The top sheet is the sauce and we spread it out. The comforter is the cheese and we cover it. The pillows are all the toppings. They have so much fun pretending they are Italian and singing songs.

TIPS:

1. Have your children teach you something new.
2. Ask for their advice on a problem.
3. Be willing to let your kids help you. No need to play 'supermom' or 'superdad'.
4. Have older kids get involved by having them write down different chores on pieces of paper, put them in a hat, and have each family member draw out three or four jobs each week. The benefit of this method is that each family member is involved and they know that they will not be stuck with the same job forever.
5. Begin family councils this week!
6. Have your child lead housecleaning and other activities. Be sure to turn on your favorite songs when cleaning, not just the kids' favorite. You will have more fun and your kids will love seeing you have fun.

Myth Six:
Parents Have to Let The Child Know Who's the Boss in the House.

When parents need to let the kids know who is the boss in the house it can keep a family from being a true team. The child may respect the parent but it will be based on fear. It also teaches the child that it is important not to let anyone boss them around. And having it their way is most important. As a result we spend a large portion of our life as adults making sure no one tells us what to do which does not lend itself to creating close and intimate relationships.

New Idea:
Parents and Kids Can Be Friends.

Walton Story by Susie

I have felt that my four sons, Adam, Nathan, Luke and Chris, and I have always been friends and I've told that to people for many years. I know that's an idea that a lot of parents have trouble with. I usually hear the reaction, "how can your kids be your friends? You're supposed to be the parent - they need to know who the parent is."

Friends - what is a friend? In Webster's Dictionary, it is, "a person you know well and regard with affection and trust. A friend is someone who provides assistance, someone you can confide in. He is a good ally." One would hope that definition matches the relationship you have with your child. One who is close to you and with whom you have affection and trust. A friend is someone that you would do basically anything for. I'm sure that is how we all feel about our children and would want our children to feel the same about us.

Teaching Point:

You can maintain being a parent, setting boundaries, disciplining, and still remain in deep connection with your child. This is basic to building a resilient family relationship. They know and understand that you love them through thick and thin. Setting boundaries with mutual respect is part of being good friends. In fact, at times saying 'no' is the most loving thing you can do for your child or friend.

Story: Mom Runs a Marathon

We often set ourselves up to NOT be supported. When I planned my marathon, I did not do that. I talked with ALL of my family members. I let them know what it would mean in regards to the commitments that I currently had with the family, commitments that may not get done or would get done at a different rate. I let them know how important running this marathon was to me and that my determination was strong.

Then I started doing the work. When my family SAW me

running on days when I didn't want to and leaving things undone when I usually didn't, they knew it was time for them to pitch in. I would come home from my run and the bed was made, dishes done, laundry started, carpooling taken care of.

My family even showed up on bikes in the middle of long runs to offer support. They were truly amazing. After a 12, 16, or 20 mile run, when my body was over heated and ready to stop, I would look up and see my husband standing there with water or tea and more importantly a look of support on his face.

When I look back on the marathon I remember my youngest daughter running across the finish line with me; my son skateboarding to find my location; my middle daughter and her friends looking in amazement at a 39-year-old MOM running a marathon; and most of all, the tremendous SUPPORT that went into accomplishing that one goal.

I learned through this experience that families are a powerful team. My physical body ran that marathon alone, but my whole self ran that race with a team behind it.

Walton Story from Luke

I remember being on a family vacation to Catalina Island with my mom and my brothers. This is something she likes to do with us every year although as we get older it's harder because we are all so busy. One day we took a two-hour hike to the beach with a picnic lunch. After eating, we looked at the map and decided to take a different trail home. Well, it was an extremely difficult hike. The first two and a half miles were straight up. I remember it was so hard for my mom that she even started crying. But we all supported each other and we would cheer as each of us made it to the top of each part of the trail. We were somewhat unbelieving when we looked up and saw yet another part of the trail going straight up. After over six hours, we finally made it back to our campsite. Even though it was really hard, we all stuck together which made it possible for us to make it.

Three Walton Stories from Nate
Story One:

I remember when I was playing basketball in high school and I hurt my ankle right before the championship game. I was so upset because I had worked my whole high school career for this state championship game and I had an injury. I remember thinking, "Oh man, I am not going to be able to play."

My mom spent 36 hours with me at the doctor's office and in the training room trying to help me get my ankle just good enough so I could play. I ended up playing just ten minutes in the game even though I was on crutches and I probably should not have. I remember my mom just sitting there by me at the game telling me its okay you are going to have your college career ahead of you. At the same time she knew how important it was to me.

Story Two:

A happy time was when my whole family was there for me when I graduated from Princeton. It was the first time that all my family was there at the same time. I got to show them what my life had been like for the last few years. They had all been there to visit me individually, but not all together and they had a couple of days to experience that with me. It was just such a great homage to me, I thought, that they were all there. And I would not have been there, graduating from Princeton, if they had not always been so supportive of me.

Story Three:

I think the best thing to do is just love your kids so much and show them that you love them. Then when you try to communicate with them they will understand that you love them. Sometimes parents think that their child knows they love him but indeed they do not. Parents should make their lives and their family so full of love that their kids grow automatically in that love.

One of the problems in our society is there is so much emphasis on keeping stoic and not sharing love with people particularly not with your kids. Sometimes people do not say the things they mean, like telling your kid how much you love him. That is why it was so great to be in our family. We never could say that we loved each other enough. This is something our grandmother, TuTu, would remind us constantly, that you can spoil kids by giving them too much stuff but you cannot spoil them by giving them too much love.

Story: I Love You

Since forever, I have been telling my sons that I love them all the time. One of the ways that I tell them is that I ask them - "What do I do to you?" The answer - "Love you." It always gets a little smile and maybe a hug. It's often best to do this when they are least expecting it. One night not long ago, I was putting my then five-year-old son to sleep for the night. I asked him "What do I do to you?" and he answered, "Love you." I then asked, "How do you know?" and he said "I just do. I've always known." Unprompted, he then said "I love you too Daddy, all the time. I love you in the morning. I love you in the afternoon. I love you at night. I even love you when you are telling me that what I am doing is not OK with you."

Story: First Love

When my son was sixteen his first love blossomed and eventually they broke up. He came into our room and we talked and cried together for a long while. He also befriended two girls who had some serious problems going on in their homes and he became an 'advisor' to them. He would always share with me and ask for my advice. He came downstairs one night after hours of conversations with one of his troubled friends and said, "It all comes down to parents. I realize how lucky I am. Thank you mom for everything you are, for being my mom and my friend." He than gave me one of his big bear hugs.

<u>Story: Love Bags</u>

I have to admit I thought it sounded a little corny at first. One day, the kids and I were all getting frustrated, so we decided to sit down and make our Love Bags. What a surprise. We all had so much fun talking about what makes us feel better (hugs, music, dancing, snacks, making silly faces). I would write down what they said or draw pictures. Even my two and a half year-old got into decorating her bag and choosing what she wanted in it.

Throughout the week, the kids would remember their Love Bags and run over to them to find just the right thing that would make them feel better. When I would get mad or frustrated, my little one would look at me and say, "Are you fustated, mama? Do you need your Love Bag?" That right there was enough to make me smile!

Walton Story by Susie

When my sons were teens they started telling dirty jokes in front of me. One day I went to them and said, "Guys, I don't feel very respected when you tell those jokes around me, so would you mind saying them somewhere else?" They just looked at me and said, "sure." They hadn't even thought about it, but that's being a true friend, letting your friends know when something is working or not working for you.

Walton Story by Susie

My boys have been asking me for a long time to write this book and I feel that, in itself, is a sign of respect and signifies the type of relationship I have with them. That's why I wanted to share some stories with you and some tools to help create that closeness within your family unit. I know when my sons were growing up, I was there a lot with them. I was fortunate to be a stay-at-home-mom, but I didn't worry about everything being perfectly clean. In fact, it kind of became a family joke, whenever anyone came to visit our house they usually ended up folding clothes with me, as there were always clothes that needed folding.

Teaching Point: Parents as Friends...

Creating a great relationship with your kids will make parenting a lot more fun. I think that one of the secrets of successful and happy parenting is being happy and having fun with your kids. There are so many ways you can learn to be your child's friend, have fun, and have a relationship of cooperation, mutual respect, and deep love. Here are some quotes from several of my nieces and nephews who have great relationships with their parents.

Katie: Age 15

"My mom and I love each other and just love hanging out together. It's just really fun to be with her. I am a very lucky person to have such a great mom."

Cindy: Age 21

"I feel my parents are my friends because I have always been able to talk with them and I can trust that they're not going to judge me based on what I said or the mistakes I make. I know that they love me no matter what. Often they will respond with, 'Oh, you're human, mistakes happen and that is okay.' I have always loved how they do not judge me or my friends when we have blown it."

Kamuela: Age 19

"My dad can understand where I'm coming from in a lot of situations, how I feel when it comes to girls or sports or whatever it might be. He has been there and done that. He can understand what I'm feeling and so I can talk to him about pretty much anything. My dad used to take us surfing all the time, we'd go on hikes, and camping too. We spent a lot of time together - me and my brothers and my dad."

Aileen: Age 17

"Because I'm in high school, I have lots of friends with issues. I can talk to my mom about things my friends do because she trusts me and knows that I'll make good decisions. Then we can worry about them together."

Woody: Age 14

"My mom, can still make lemonade for me and joke around with me. I can tell her jokes, even gross jokes, and she won't say, "that's disgusting," or ground me or any thing. My mom can say silly things too and that makes her seem more like a friend. She just likes to joke around and I can always talk to her. My dad likes to take me places, and we are like best friends because we go to McDonalds and talk and eat food and stuff. He's lots of fun and we like to go camping and stuff like that."

Teaching Point:

A great way of connecting with your kids is reading. Spend time reading with them every night or play cards, or board games. Let's spend a few minutes talking about board games. They are hardly in existence anymore. We used to play Monopoly, Parchesi, and Chutes and Ladders. Discovery Toys has some incredible board games today, like Enchanted Forest. This is something that can be a lifelong family activity.

Walton Story by Susie:

Luke used to set up four or five board games across the floor and we would go from game to game playing. He is such a gamer. He just loves board games. He would just play them and play them and his brothers and I would all play too. To this day, when we all get together, there we are playing Scategories.

One summer we went on a family vacation to Sedona and what did we do every night? Pull out Monopoly and we'd play it until someone ran out of money or until someone got mad and would throw the board upside down. That's happened a few times in our family! Trust me.

Being a close-knit family does not mean that we are the Brady Bunch Clan and we're all getting along. There have been plenty of arguments in this family, plenty of yelling at each other, plenty of throwing the board upside down because one is not winning.

That's part of life guys, the ups and downs of life. **You cannot expect your kids to behave at school, home and everywhere else all the time.** They've got all the time to let it out somewhere, so it might as well be at home. It can be a wonderful time for learning different ways of handling conflict.

TIPS:

1. Next time you get home late and making dinner will be stressful, pull out a tablecloth and put it on the kitchen floor or backyard lawn. Bring out the peanut butter and jelly and bread, some carrot strips or fruit and have yourselves an instant picnic.

2. During the summer, go to the beach or park once a week for a family picnic.

3. Get out blankets and make some popcorn and have a family movie night.

4. Play cards or a board game tonight.

5. Ask your family members to support you in accomplishing a goal you set.

6. Breathe.

7. Have fun!

Myth Seven:
Experts Know Best About Your Child.

As parents, especially with our first-born, we depend too much on what the experts tells us is best for our kids. It is good to get as much information as you can about raising your children and teens, and then do what you truly feel is best for your child or family. Example: There are many experts that say 'spare the rod...spoil the child' and that spanking is okay if done under control. Well, I can tell you there is not an inch of respect in hitting another human being and there are definitely alternatives to using spanking as a mode of discipline! And by the way, if the sheep were ever hit with the rod, they would have gone crazy and ran away.

New Idea:
Follow Your Heart.

Story: The Art Therapist

I lost my husband in the 9/11 tragedy. Our daughter Mikki was four-years-old. When Mikki was nine-years-old, I was at a conference and met a woman who said she was an art therapist. She asked if I had anything I wanted her to interpret and so I showed her a picture Mikki had drawn for me just before I left to go to the conference. Mikki had told me it was a picture of me giving birth to her and her father was in the picture with her teddy bear, which she still has! I showed it to this woman and here is a list of what she said:

1. Your daughter is very connected to her father.
2. There is no connection to you.
3. His eyebrows represent wisdom.
4. He has a face.
5. She has a face.
6. You do not have a face and your head and arms are black.
7. She does not know who you are and wants her mom back.
8. She is nine.. there are nine legs on the table.
9. Teddy bear represents past lives. She and your husband, Don, were connected in past lives. He is in the Spirit World now and not in her present.

The art therapist then proceeded to ask why I was so angry. I did not even know I was angry. I sat there in shock and extreme pain because it made no sense. Mikki and I have always been very close. My therapist, who has known me for five years, happened to also be at the conference and she took one look at me and pulled me aside. I told her the story and told her how confused I felt because I thought Mikki and I were very connected. What this woman said did not feel correct. I showed my therapist the picture and this is what she said, "The picture is a paradox. You separate from people who are leaving in order to decrease the pain and Mikki picked up on this and drew a picture mirroring what it is you do. Actually, you and Mikki really are very connected." I felt so much better after that and learned a very valuable lesson about always weighing what the experts say with what I feel in my heart.

Story: Taking the High Road

When Katie was 11 her school suggested that I put her on Ritalin during the school hours as she was having a difficult time focusing. To know Katie is to love Katie. She is a spirited, loving and fun daughter. Medicating her just did not seem RIGHT as I have always loved her enthusiasm for life. So, I did some research and decided to have her attend Brain Highways and to begin taking blue green algae, a food supplement from Cell Tech. I also spoke to her about what she could do to help focus and she decided to wear a ring that she would twirl on her finger when the teacher was talking in order to help her focus. Katie is now 15 and is doing great. Thank goodness my heart spoke loudly and I did what I knew would be best for my child.

Teaching Point:

Refer to Myth 17 for more tools on kinesthetic learning.

Story: The Family Bed

Our son is three-years-old. He has been sick frequently in his young life and has had multiple surgeries. Lately, he has been waking up scared during the night and wanting to sleep with us. As he is our first-born, we started asking people for advice. What we were hearing was that it is important that he stays in his room, do not give in as you will never get him out of your bed. Well, we were having many sleepless nights and everyone was unhappy and grumpy. I was telling Susie about my dilemma and she said what ever my heart was feeling would be the best for me! I said to get some sleep. When she asked if we could sleep when he was in bed with us, we said yes. So, at that point, we realized it was best for all of us to create a family bed. We can happily report we are getting a good night's sleep now and what a difference that has made for all of us!

Story: A Journey of the Heart

I have two ten-year-old sons. I want to share what I have gone through in the last few years with doctors diagnosing them with ADD and how I chose alternative ways of handling that, as a result of following my heart. Due to difficulty in school, they were tested and it showed they had ADD. I could see that they were very distractible and, of course, I was really sad and felt guilty at times wondering what I did wrong. I found out it is hereditary and that it may have something to do with them being preemies. They suggested medication for them. I just couldn't see seven-year-olds being put on meth-amphetamines. It was emotional, the boys were so young, they didn't even have a sense of their own bodies yet.

I listened to a very well-known expert at an all-day workshop who knew a lot about ADD. He talked about all the medications and the testing they do with brain waves. That day, as I sat eating lunch with my sisters, I said, "I can't do this" even though they were pushing me to do this testing and get them on the drugs. For a long time it was just heart-wrenching to go through and to think about my decision.

I decided to try biofeedback which seemed to helped them with self-control so they could bring themselves back down and be more in control instead of being in complete rage. We started therapy, discipline therapy, and parenting courses. It was a struggle and it was hard. Patience. Crying. Drinking. It's was also hard on the marriage. I don't know how we kept the family together.

I realized after a while to stop talking to my family about it. I was depressed and sad because of the disrespect and the outrages from the kids. It was a combination I think of the ADD and their being little immature boys. But, I just couldn't do it. There was nothing inside of me that said to put them on medication.

Finally I got support from my family and I said, "This is my decision and this is what I want to do." My husband was also supportive of this decision. There has been improvement. They also started yoga. That's helped them learn about their bodies, focusing, and being internal. It has taken about a year and a half, but they're bringing it into their world now. They will lie on the floor sometimes doing an exercise. Once I saw them sitting down and using "Om" to calm themselves down. That was really cool. And they're constantly saying, "deep breath." Yoga is like a foundation for home. They've got things to fall back on and work with. When they're 15 or 16 years-old and they know what's going on with them, they may say, "Mom, I need more help and maybe I need medication." At least then they will have a sense of what's going on and we could discuss that. But, at this young age, I couldn't do it.

I believe giving the boys choices has been very helpful. Detaching has also been very helpful. Just sitting down and talking about things, learning how to communicate with them and helping them understand and express their feelings has helped. When there is a problem we go back and we make sure it is cleaned up and holes aren't left - turning a mistake into a teachable moment.

A valuable tool has been logical and natural consequences. If I give a consequence really fast because I'm angry, they'll tell me "Mom, that's not related." So then I will back up and come up with one that is related. They may not be happy with it but they can live with it.

I have also learned to apologize for the wrong things I've done and the wrong things I've said. This has made the relationship much better. I use make-ups to model for them and they are now using them. If they have damaged the other one's toy, they are responsible for paying for it or fixing it.

My suggestion to parents who have been told by the schools that their kids have ADDHD or ADD and that they need medication is to follow your gut feeling and get plenty of information and explore alternatives.

Perhaps some parents are choosing medication because they're both working and they don't have time to deal with it or they are not aware of other alternatives. You have to be willing to spend a lot of time. I did a lot of research on the internet, just looking for natural ways. I did a lot of natural stuff. I wasn't able to change their diet, because they are just picky little eaters. But I have a feeling it would have helped. So I suggest the diet. I have talked to some parents who said it really made a big difference. I have partially eliminated dyes and limit the sugars and especially corn syrup.

To me, using medication on my sons would have been like putting a band-aid on a burn. My kids don't know themselves well enough. It's like squashing a personality to me. I don't know, maybe they'd do better in school. It was such a hard decision. Even at this time I feel they're smart. Most children with ADD are very smart. I could be holding them back a little bit because they could probably excel very far in school, even further, but I have to look at the whole person. They are learning how to deal with it. For us, it is working. Our sons are alive and alert and the family is constantly learning.

Teaching Point:

Some people say that once kids are on these drugs they stop growing emotionally. So, they may be growing in the academic world but they are basically stunting their emotional intelligence.

Others feel that a lot of the ADD/ADHD symptoms come from anxiety ridden children who for example are pressured at age one and a half or two to use the toilet. They are being brought into this world full of stress thinking they have to perform for rewards and external gratification.

So parents, slow down a bit and let your kids be kids. As I often tell my students, your children will more than likely be potty-trained by the time they go to college. If you let them decide when they are ready, without rewards and bribes, you will be giving them an incredible gift of self-management at a very early age.

TIPS:

1. When you make a decision about your child, follow your heart. Do your homework and find support. Remember, it takes a village to raise a child.

2. Take three breaths into your heart area and think about the decision you are making. If your heart area expands then it is the right decision for you. If it constricts then it is best you come up with another option.

3. Slow down, when you are relaxed your children will be relaxed too. We live in such a busy world and when we are in that busy mode we lose out on so many positive experiences with our kids.

4. Have fun!

5. Breathe.

Myth Eight:
Kids Don't do Well in
Single-Parent Homes.

Single families have received a bad reputation. I know there are statistics showing the problems kids from single families face. I also know, from being divorced for the past 18 years, it need not be a hindrance to raising healthy, secure, happy kids. If the parent is secure and happy, then the kids will model the same behavior. In a divorce, it is best to support the other parent as best as you can.

For example: When my sons first started going back and forth between two houses they would call from their dad's and complain that they were not allowed to watch TV and would I come and pick them up? I acknowledged how they were feeling and asked what else they could do besides watch TV. Soon after that they quit calling as much to complain because more often than not I would acknowledge their feelings without trying to fix the problem. I knew they were capable of figuring out other options and I knew that their dad had their best interest in mind.

Now, I am not talking about abusive situations. I am speaking about the everyday little things kids can complain about whether you are in a one-parent household or two. In the case where there is just one parent it is most important that the parent takes care of themself, allowing them to be the best parent possible. If you are in this situation, don't try to take the place of both parents because you will drive yourself crazy and lose out on the fun of being a parent.

New Idea:
A Great Family Can Exist with One Parent and as Few as One Child.

Story: Jen and Jordie

I am a single parent who has been through a marriage and divorce within my son, Jordin's, lifespan. Jordin's biological father has never been involved in his life. We have a strong mother-son bond and a fantastic friendship as we rely on each other for support - both in daily tasks and emotionally. We have achieved a balance that works for us and we are not shy about expressing what we need from each other.

I had Jordin take on responsibilities at a young age to help me out and also to teach him a good work ethic. At age seven he was cleaning the bathroom on Saturday mornings. As he got older, I gave him additional responsibilities such as packing his own lunch, biking to and from school, and taking the city bus to get to soccer practice. These responsibilities have given him a real appreciation for the daily things mothers do all the time for their children. Living with a single parent, he understands that he has to pitch in if I'm not going to be burnt out by the time I get home from work. I have found our relationship to be based on teamwork and very open channels of communication. We have been through many ups and downs together and this has made our bond even stronger.

Story: Lily

After my wife passed away, my three-year-old daughter, Lily, started having intense angry outbursts. She would lose control and be filled with anger. I knew we needed help. Thank God for a bad tooth of mine! The person who crafted my tooth referred me to Susie Walton. It has made all the difference in the world bringing peace and harmony to our lives. I learned how my daughter's acting out was really her call for attention. It has also made me more aware, so I can be proactive.

For example, if I am talking on the phone or with a friend and she wants my attention, I immediately respond by rubbing her back, enabling me to continue my conversation. I am able to recognize when she is in a power role and I can redirect the situation. There is no yelling in our home. I personally love the practice of the encouragement feast as it creates a connection between us and sets us in our hearts.

When I am doing paperwork or any chore and she wants me to play with her, we come up with a win-win solution. For example, we play together for ten minutes then I will go back to work. The interesting part is she stops playing even before the ten minutes are up. It is truly a win-win. I am also big on giving Lily choices, as I want to work together instead of just telling her what to do. **I look at it like I am parenting with intention and not just reacting.**

Through all the adversity we have been through together around the death of her mother, we truly have a special bond. There is not a lack of love or laughter in our house. Every evening we sing as loud as we can to a CD that Lily picks out (for some reason she likes Steely Dan). We also go on adventure walks where Lily does most of the talking. That one-on-one time really sets a tone and creates a strong bond.

Story: Letting our Kids Support Us

A single mom went back to school and had to devote a fair amount of time to her studies. She had set a goal to pass a big exam. Her child asked how he could support her and she said he could quiz her on some of the questions. So the child quizzed his mom and enjoyed being the support rather than being the one supported. It was something that was important and worked. The mom passed her test.

Teaching Point:

When we let our kids see how valuable they are to us it increases their self-esteem and they get to experience how important they are in the family constellation.

Story: We are Family

A single-parent dad who is a teacher took the parenting class. He has two young teenage daughters. They live in an affluent area and a lot of the kids in school could buy clothes whenever they wanted. The girls were asking their dad for more money to buy clothes. He kept saying, "I don't have it." The girls were 13 and 15 at this time, so what he said to them was, "Why don't you balance the checkbook for a month and if after a month you can figure out where there's some extra money, then I'd be willing to talk about giving you some more money for extra clothes."

After one month of balancing the checkbook, these girls became aware that their dad did not have the extra money, and as a result, they started babysitting more in order to buy their own clothes. If you don't have the money, then the kids need to know that, not to make them feel bad, but just to have them be aware. This is for older teenage kids. One way to help kids learn about money management and monetary decisions is to give them an allowance to manage.

TIPS:

1. Be willing to get help from your kids.
2. Take care of yourself. Do not try to over-compensate for the other parent.
3. Make a meal together or play a game together.
4. Ask for support from family and friends.
5. Remember, it takes a village to raise a child.
6. Breathe.
7. Have fun!

Myth Nine:
Family Vacations and Outings are a Hassle or Too Expensive.

Family vacations and outings can be a hassle and stressful especially if you do not create a team in the family and allow the kids to have a say in what is to take place. One of the biggest problems with family vacations or outings is trying to pack in too many things in too short a time. It is important to give more value to time spent together versus how much you do. Some of our best vacations have included a hike in the morning and spending the rest of the day playing cards and board games, and of course, having a lot of good food.

New Idea:
Visualize How You Want Your Family to Be and Make it Happen!!

Story: Family Campout

It is important to have quality family time without the expense. Each year we look forward to our family camping trip. The kids help decide where to go, and help pack the equipment. When we arrive at the site, the real quality time begins. As a family we set up the tent, cut the firewood, make the fires, cook the food, hike, play games, and have a great time being a family team.

Story: Make Someone Else More Important

Several years ago we took our two boys, Alistair and Toby, to Seattle and Vancouver for our summer vacation. We often visit Vancouver, as their dad and I spent our teenage years growing up there and our families and many friends still live there. Unfortunately, having so many people we each want to see and many places that all four of us hold dear and want to visit often causes conflict about how to spend our time. The boys want to go to Playdium (a noisy arcade); we want to have some nice dinners out with friends. Ed wants to get in several rounds of disc golf; I want to spend long leisurely evenings playing Scrabble with my Mom. Somehow, in the past, vacations seemed to deteriorate to bickering and power struggles and in the end no one got what they really wanted which was to have fun together. I was determined that this year would be different!

So, on our three-hour drive north from Seattle, I asked everyone what they wanted to do while we were in Vancouver. We made a huge list that took up two pages! There were more things than we could possibly do in a week! Beside each activity, I placed the initial of anyone that wanted to participate. There were things we all wanted to do like visit the gelato store that has over a hundred flavors. There were things only one, or two or three of us wanted to participate in. When the list was complete and no one could think of anything else to put on it, I asked each person to name their top three priorities in order. Ok, so now we had a plan. How were we going to make sure that we stayed focused on doing all the fun things?

I sat and thought and thought and then I remembered a friend saying, "What would the world be like and how would you behave differently if you KNEW that no matter what you did or what happened there were five people who would definitely be there for you?" Could the answer be hidden in this thought? And then it dawned on me. If each of us was responsible for someone ELSE getting to do the things they wanted then we would be much more generous in our planning, much less desperate in our demands. It would add a sense of mystery and curiosity about how and when activities would unfold. The key was KNOWING that your desires would absolutely be handled.

So we set up a wheel. I was responsible for my youngest son, who was in turn responsible for my husband. Ed was responsible for our oldest son who planned activities for me. After a fairly short brainstorming session to wrinkle out all the "what ifs", everyone seemed eager to arrive in Vancouver to start.

What happened next was amazing. I had put on my list "Check out Crescent Beach" (a large sand beach south of Vancouver where I thought we might someday relocate). It was my number two priority. Almost immediately, Alistair realized that he could be sure that my number two was handled if we stopped there on the way to town. No objections. In fact, everyone started pitching in ideas to make the stop really fun. "Let's get ice cream." "Let's go for a walk and a swim." We were having a blast together.

When we got to Vancouver it was dinnertime. We all sat down and talked about what kind of food we wanted to eat (food is important in our family). The boys were committed to Italian. Suddenly Toby piped up "Number three on Dad's list is visiting an Italian restaurant downtown." I could see that we were heading towards an impasse.

I knew the Italian restaurant Ed wanted to visit was fancy and my boys didn't like to wear anything dressier than a t-shirt! "No problem" they said, and "by the way, Mom, would you iron my shirt!" I was sure this couldn't last. We went to the Italian restaurant all dressed up. The owner took such great care of us. He even made special dishes for Toby.

All week long the same theme played out. The boys would get up in the morning and figure out that these two people can do a particular activity while those two do something they want, then we'll meet here and this one can go off and do their thing while the other three do this, and on the way to the first activity we can stop here and handle this request, and on and on. It was like having a scavenger hunt. The challenge was fitting in everything each of us wanted to do.

The night before we left town, we got out our list, now dog-eared, crossed out, highlighted and took inventory. We had done everyone's first, second and third choices. Those had been handled or scheduled in the first two days. We had done almost everything on the list! In fact we agreed that we had done everything on the list that we had really wanted to do. No regrets. And the best part was that we had felt cared about, we had shared joyous times, we had learned interesting things about each other's skills and desires and we had come together as a family team, all working on the common goal of mutual joy and happiness.

Looking back, I think that may have been the last vacation we took as a foursome. Alistair got old enough to work and couldn't come when we went on our next vacation. I'm glad that we had that time. We each experienced the joy of caring for someone else, and for the group, more than ourselves and knowing that is when your needs are truly handled.

Story: Off to Scotland!!

Family Meetings are a great time for families to create goals and share dreams. In one family with four kids, the youngest, age 12, wanted to visit castles. They decided to make that a family goal. For a year this family saved their money, didn't go out much, babysat more, and in one year this family of six was in Scotland visiting castles. A goal can be anything and when you put the energy of a family behind it, trust me, good things can and will happen.

Walton Story by Susie

We had a family reunion at the beach in Balboa when the boys were in their early teens. Balboa has a great fun zone full of games and rides and we all like to spend lots of time (and money) there. At a family meeting about six months before the reunion, we talked about the fun zone and how to have enough money to have a blast. We decided to put a big jar in the kitchen and every time anyone had change to throw it in. It was amazing how much money accumulated to spend in the fun zone. I think it was even more fun because the boys knew they had made it happen with their plan.

Story: Airplane Bliss

My two sons and I have traveled a great deal together. We traveled to Hawaii when they were three and five-years-old and India, Hong Kong, and Japan when they were eight and ten years-old. Inevitably, toward the end of our flights people would comment on how well my children behaved on these long plane rides. They asked my secret. I told them that we would discuss the trip way ahead of time and I would ask the boys what they needed to take with them to be happy and content. They each had a small backpack they filled with quiet games, books, snacks, and toys (this was before the age of DVD players and gameboys). It was always a joy to travel with them and because of working together as a team the possibilities were endless on where we could travel.

Walton Story by Susie

My sons and I have been going on yearly family vacations for many years now. At first I took on the major responsibility of the planning, organizing, and carrying it through. It is very cool that in the last several years my sons have taken on a large part of all of the vacation planning. This makes it even more fun for me and I can see it has become a tradition that hopefully they will carry on with their families.

TIPS:

1. Use a Family Council to create a vacation.
2. Let each family member choose one thing to do during the vacation.
3. Plan a vacation at a state park. It is rather inexpensive and the outdoors does wonders to one's soul and mind.
4. Make Vision Boards of your proposed vacation. (Cut and paste pictures from magazines on a poster board that illustrate your vacation vision.)
5. Breathe.
6. And of course, have fun!

Myth Ten:
Children are Too Young to Resolve Fights and They Need Time Outs!!

You could spend most of your parenting career refereeing fights which does not create a very calm household. Your kids could grow up to believe they do not have to utilize self control or take responsibility for their fights as you or someone else will step in.

Example: My youngest son would often get in arguments with his brothers. One day I asked him why he did this. His response was, "because it is fun and I know if I yell loud enough you will come in and stop it!"

The problem with Time Outs is that they are usually done in an angry and/or threatening tone. The child either learns to blame others or to be angry with you and not be accountable for his or her actions.

Self-quieting on the other hand teaches kids internal management and control. We all need time alone so why make it a punishment. Here are some stories of families who have been able to reduce fighting and teach their children how to manage their own self-quieting.

New Idea:
Teach Children Conflict Resolution and Self-Calming Time.

Story: Full-time Referee Takes a Vacation

I found that I was constantly acting as a referee between my two children. I would pick a side based on what I saw (or what I thought I saw), and make a decision. Susie made me rethink this whole process. How would they solve their problems if I wasn't around? What if I didn't see everything that happened and made a choice based on wrong information? What I want for my children is to help them grow into decision makers, problem solvers and negotiators. What better way to prepare them for an adult life?

Since they are four-and-a-half and two-and-a-half, I initially helped them come up with many different solutions to their problems. They decided together which one would work best for them. Eventually, they were able to come up with solutions on their own. They didn't always choose the one I thought would work best, but they chose the one that worked best for both of them. By encouraging the kids to work out solutions on their own, I find they are better able to play together and work through problems that arise. Sometimes when I hear them arguing, I'll ask if there is a problem. The answer I usually get back now is, "We're working it out!" It definitely is empowering for them.

There seemed to be daily struggles with, "it's mine!" in our house. Now when this happens, I'll acknowledge them both with a rub on the back and I'll hold out my hand for the item. After what sometimes seems like an eternity, the toy is usually handed over. Then I use the call out phrase, "when you two decide how to share this, let me know. I'll have it in the kitchen with me. I know you can work it out." Initially I got a lot of protests and crying. We would sometimes spend time thinking of solutions like using a timer, taking turns or playing with something else. Now if they start to fight over an item, I'll start walking toward them and one of them usually shouts out, "Let's use the timer!"

Story: Self-Quieting Bag versus the 'Naughty Pad'

My six-year-old and nine-year-old have grown up with 'self calming places'. Since we are not always at home when we need the self-calming place we have created 'calming bags'. My artistic daughter filled hers with paper, crayons, scissors, coloring books, glitter glue, and books. My kinesthetic son has silly putty, play dough, etch-a-sketch, ropes, strings to tie knots and more. They both have two pages in their bags, one to help them express their feelings (called the 'I feel page') and another to help them identify their own part in the problem. They suggested I have one too. My calming bag includes candles, incense, crocheting stuff, a book, perfume, and bubble bath as my favorite calming place is the bath tub. My son reminded me to add the 'I feel page' in there too.

Teaching Point:

Make copies of a simple conflict resolution guide to use when your kids are having an argument. On it you will put the following information:

I Feel: _____
I Want: _____
How can we make this work for both of us?

When using this visual aid, have each of the kids express what they are feeling and what they want and then together have them come up with a solution that works for both of them. You can coach them, but be sure they are speaking directly to each other and not to you. This is something that all children and adults can use when resolving conflict or problem-solving in a respectful and very effective way. If one of the children is too young to speak, have the older child be the spokesperson for the two of them. Copies posted in their rooms and on the refrigerator are great reminders. Carry one in your car too!

Story: Using the Conflict Resolution out in the World

My six year old daughter gets overwhelmed and scared when other kids roar in her face, like some boys did while playing dinosaurs. Even though she has been practicing using win-win statements at home by telling her brother how she feels when he gets too aggressive, she didn't think about it with the new boys in class. After she came to me crying, I reminded her to use her "win-win." She went right back to the boys and said, "I get scared when you roar in my face. I want you to be more quiet next to me or roar over there instead." The boys happily roared elsewhere and she got a great chance to practice asking for what she wanted.

Story: Self-Quieting at School

We have been using self-quieting with our five-year-old son Marino for about two years. At home, he usually just goes in his room and builds with his blocks to cool off, he also has a small tent full of pillows if he wants to use it. Recently he was upset when we were driving, and he decided to just put a blanket over his head to make a self-quieting space -- it worked great and I told him how I admired his ability to get himself centered and calm.

One day after that his kindergarten teacher pulled me aside to tell me how impressed she was with how he handled his anger in class. Apparently he got upset with her about having to follow directions for an art project, and used angry words. When she said that the way he spoke to her wasn't okay with her, he said he needed some quiet time, went over to the mat on his own, and just sat for a while. When he came back, he was polite and calm.

Being accustomed to directing children to do anything like

that, she was very impressed he did it on his own. We shared a bit about our techniques with her. Marino made sure to talk about one of his favorite things, the love bags. She created a class *love* box to which all the children contributed suggestions: a minute on the beanbag chair, a minute sitting next to the teacher, a minute of coloring, a story, a hug. Now when a student is sad or upset, he or she has the option of getting something out of the love box in addition to the more traditional classroom management tools in place.

Story: Working it Out

My three-year-old son and five-year-old daughter share a room. They usually wake up before me and play in their room until I get up. Some mornings they will get into a fight, which will wake me up and I'll have to intervene to get them to work it out. I will try to get them to resolve conflicts on their own, but usually at this stage with my three-year-old I have to walk him through it. One morning last week, my daughter informed me that they had gotten into a fight and had hit each other. She said they then stopped the fighting and gave each other hugs as a make-up and worked it out on their own.

Story: Self-Quieting and Self-Management go Hand-In-Hand

We talked to the boys about choosing a quiet place to blow off steam. Jack chose his bed. When he threw temper tantrums, hit, yelled, or got down from the table while eating, we consistently told him that wasn't the way we acted in our family, set him in his quiet place, and told him to rejoin us when he was ready. One night at dinner he told us that he didn't like what we had to eat and he got very angry with us. He got down from the table and said, "I am going to my quiet place."

Story: Rabbit House

My daughter, Lydia (age three) went to Disneyland for the first time. One ride she admired was Alice in Wonderland. Then, Lydia saw the Tea Cup ride. Everybody loves the Tea Cups! On the pathway between the two rides, Lydia came across a small door to a small house painted on the side of a building. Lydia said, "Mommy, this must be Rabbit's House." Imagine how many children have stumbled across this same little door.

A few months later, I was digging in the hall closet under the stairs frantically searching through boxes stored in the closet. It was tax-season, and I needed to find a document to complete our IRS 1040 tax return. A big mess spilled over into the hallway and into the living room. Lydia asked me what I was doing. She joined me in the small hall closet, laughing, and asking lots of questions. Lydia thought this was terribly fun and exciting as I was making a big mess. Wrapping paper, tennis racquets, an old walking cane, and a plastic hat for St. Patrick's Day, were just a few of the treasures Lydia picked up and admired. Once I stepped out of the closet with a large plastic storage box, Lydia discovered she could see deeper into the closet. "Hey, what's back there, Mommy?" Lydia asked. Lydia was thrilled. Behind the boxes and hanging ski clothes was a small space under the steps. It was a space adults could only squeeze into if they got down on their hands and knees. It went back deep too. As she looked back Lydia pronounced, "Mommy, it looks like Rabbit's House!"

The following week, I attended a parenting class. The subject that night was changing "time-outs" from a punitive measure, to a "self-quieting" area. Susie, the instructor, explained the concept as a place for children go to and regain their composure. Both the child and parent needed to "take a break." This location should be one that the child selects verses the traditional command, "You need a time-out. Go to your room!" Susie advised the parents this new self-quieting location should also be utilized when the child is happy and calm. The location should be filled with items that would help a child "break-out" of her tantrum and to self-calm.

Well, this was a new concept for me. However, while Lydia was taking a bubble bath the next evening, we discussed "time-outs." I explained, "Sometimes we yell at each other and I send you to your room for a time-out, right?" Lydia said, "Yes." "And, sometimes you are angry, too. You yell and scream at me, right?" Again, Lydia replied with a confident, "Yes." "Well, I learned that when that happens we should both take a break so that we can get calm. After we calm down, we can then talk about the problem together. Do you like that idea, Lydia?" Lydia looked up from her bath toys and said, "OK, Mommy."

I gave her the choice of where she would like to go for this "new self-calming time." I said, "Would you like to go to your room, or go to 'Rabbit's House'?" Lydia immediately selected "Rabbit's House!" The following week, Lydia and I fixed-up "Rabbit's House." Lydia selected several favorite stuffed animals, her hula skirt, a few Princess Barbie dolls, crayons and a few books. I hung a mirror on one wall, and taped photos as wallpaper on another wall. Princess foamy stickers were stuck on the outside entryway to "Rabbit's House." A framed photo of Lydia in front of the small door at Disneyland sat on top of an old Victoria's Secret hat-box, now serving as a desk. Lydia's father and sister both thought the space reminded them of Harry Potter's living space under the steps in the first book and movie. After observing the happiness it gave Lydia, they both accepted the idea. We all agreed that the door needed to remain open, and the closet light on. In addition, we purchased a battery-operated camping lantern for extra lighting. The following week,

Lydia began to misbehave. I began to lose my composure and I could feel myself getting angry with Lydia so I said to Lydia, "Go to Rabbit's House and come back when you are calmer." Lydia gave that some thought, and went. Guess what? IT WORKED!

TIPS:
1. Make a copy of the conflict resolution handout and begin using it today.
2. Make a date with your kids to create a self-quieting place.
3. Make a self-quieting place for yourself too!
4. Have the kids make self-calming bags to use when they are in the car or when traveling.
5. Breathe and Have Fun!

Second Children Always Make the First Child Jealous Resulting in Sibling Rivalry.

Often we hear that a second child creates a lot of tension and misbehavior for the first born. Sibling rivalry is probably one of the biggest complaints I hear from parents about in my parenting classes.

New Idea:
A New Child in the House can be Seen as a Gift and Siblings can be Great Friends.

Teaching Point:

Here are some things to do and not to do when you are dealing with siblings:

1. Be sure to keep both kids in the same boat. Do not take sides. You never know how it really started even if you see one hit the other. It takes two to tangle and they both need to learn how to handle conflict in constructive ways.

2. Be sure not to compare siblings. They each have their own gifts. Think of them as different plants with different needs, wants, and styles. Your job as the parent is to figure out what they each need individually and nurture that in each of them.

3. Let them express their positive and negative feelings

about their siblings when alone with you. Remember that feelings expressed lose their destructive charge. Feelings that are repressed will come out later in a much more explosive manner.

4. Have the older child teach the younger child a new skill or game and have the older child help you with the younger kids.

Walton Story by Susie

One night I was saying good night to my son, who was about fourteen at the time. I said, "Good night, I love you." He replied, "I love you too but I hate my brother, (sixteen at the time)." With curiosity, I said, "How come?" He replied, "He is always wearing my clothes and I never get to wear his." I then said, "Is there anything else you are mad at?" He said, "Yes, he is always in my room and I never get to go in his room." So then I asked, "Is there anything else?" He said, "No, good night, I love you." He went to sleep peacefully no longer angry at his brother. He just needed to get it off his chest.

Story: Conflict Resolution

I have two girls ages three and six. They generally get along, but they do bicker and compete with each other. I think the six-year-old is jealous that the three-year-old doesn't have to go to school everyday like she does and she wonders what we are doing all that time without her. The main item they bicker about is when my six-year-old tries to "lead" the younger one in play and be the boss of her. When this happens my younger child will tend to get frustrated and physically retaliate and then they are both upset and crying.

There are two things I learned from the class that can get them back on the right track. First I will ask them to do a win-win. I will ask the older one how she feels and what she wants and then do the same with the younger. For example the older one will say I am mad and hurt and I don't want you to hit me anymore. Then the younger one will say I am mad at you for telling me what to do and I want you to let me be in charge. Then I will let them talk about how they can play differently so that they are both happy. Sometimes they can work it out and continue, sometimes they choose to play a different game and sometimes they choose to play apart. In the end, I let them decide and try not to get involved. It usually ends with a makeup hug and kiss.

We have also been working really hard at helping our two children develop a close relationship. What has really helped is that we always try to put them in the same boat and we do a lot of "win-win negotiating." Because of this, we have been able to avoid many of the battles typically associated with sibling rivalry and our children are becoming really good friends.

Story: Double Dethronement

When I was five weeks pregnant, my three-year-old daughter Acadia came to me and said "Mom, I don't have a baby in my tummy" and I said, "No? Who does?" She replied "You do. It's a brother and a sister." I went out that day and bought a couple of pregnancy tests to confirm what Acadia already knew. All of them came back positive. For the next several weeks Acadia talked about her brother and her sister and I remembered that when we were contemplating trying for a second baby, I had asked Acadia "Would you like to have a baby brother or a baby sister?" and she said "Yes." And I said "Well, you'll have to choose because you are only going to get one." And she patiently replied "I want a brother and a sister."

The time we found out we were pregnant again, my husband and I had been deciding on a new car. As we went car shopping, Acadia would point out which cars would fit her brother and sister. We finally decided to put off the decision of which car to buy until we had our first pre-natal visit – I actually said to my husband "Acadia thinks we're having twins, so let's wait to buy this car until after our midwife appointment next week."

We met with our midwife and during the entire visit kept making jokes about making sure that we only had one baby. When she looked for the heartbeat using her gadget and couldn't find one, she said "Let's do an ultrasound to make sure there is only one baby in there." And said "I don't know why I said that, I never say that." She immediately told Phil to sit down – we had two babies! We were thrilled, and overwhelmed at the same time. When we told Acadia about the twins she said "I know. I asked God for a brother and a sister." At every ultrasound we printed pictures of the babies, and Acadia took them to school to show everyone "my babies."

After the babies were born, she was so proud of them, and when we would go out in public and people would marvel at the twins, she would say "they are my babies, I asked for them." We've had special moments at the dinner table with the whole family laughing at one of the twins' antics, and Acadia would look at me full of love and pride and say "Mom, you're welcome that I asked for them." From the moment she knew these babies had been conceived, she has seen these siblings as the greatest gift. Our family is full of joy and learning and growing thanks to the gift Acadia brought to all of us.

Story: Hands are for Hugging

When our daughter, Callie, came along we prepared Garret with all our new information. I am sure it helped, but nevertheless this little 'king' was dethroned. When Callie was about 17 months-old she began experimenting with hitting

Garrett and tried it often. To my surprise, Garret didn't hit back. He would say "hands are for hugging, loving, and eating. I still love you, but I don't like it when you hit me!" This is a child who just turned four-years-old; calm, patient, and loving to the little girl who dethroned him.

Story: Number Three Child

We recently became pregnant with our third boy. We are due in December. Once we found out the gender of the baby, we had a "family meeting" - and we told them about the coming baby. We talked to them about how they felt, whether they wanted a boy or a girl, and what would happen when the baby came, etc. Our eldest (now six) really seemed into it and the little guy (now three) was excited as well. About two weeks later, the eldest said he had some ideas and sat down to talk to both of us about his idea. He told us that we were going to need a lot of things for the baby and then he proceeded to list off all the things he thought we would need - bottles, blankets, diapers, wipes, bibs, little clothes, baby toys and the like. It was a very well thought out list. We told him that we liked his ideas and we wanted to make sure the baby had these things. We asked him how we could remember and he said we could write a list. He then went, got a piece of paper and pencil and wrote it all out. He is participating in our new gift.

Story: Gavin Gives His New Brother a Name

Gavin had just turned two-years-old when we knew we were

having a new baby boy and I was beginning to show. We talked to Gavin about having a new baby brother and showed him my growing tummy. My husband and I talked about names and decided on three that we both liked. We then decided to let Gavin make the final decision on the name. So we told him the three names and asked which he thought was best. He chose Benjamin. He also began to talk to Benjamin in my tummy and tell him how he was looking forward to meeting him and teaching him how to play trains with him.

By the time Benjamin arrived, Gavin was pretty accustomed to the idea, but it was still different from the reality of the situation. Allowing Gavin to talk about his negative feelings with mom or dad who were not quite as available as they used to be was very helpful. Having him help with the baby was also a great way to keep him involved and it was a big help too. It seems that often I would be in the middle of changing Benjamin's diaper and I would realize I did not have the wipes or the baby powder. Gavin was usually happy to get these for me.

The next big hurdle was when Benjamin became mobile enough to move around and mess up all of Gavin's toys and trains. Once again, letting Gavin share his anger and frustration with us was very helpful for him and us. We also asked what he thought he could do differently to keep some of his lego creations, train tracks, and log houses in tact. Some of his ideas where to build them up high or when Benjamin was asleep and put them up when he woke up. He had actually begun to call his brother Godzilla, which seemed pretty harsh.

I asked Susie what I could do to help them be more friendly to each other. She suggested I let him come up with a special game just for him and Benjamin to play. He decided on blocks. They also enjoy playing rolling ball games together. Now that Benjamin is just over a year and walking, the boys play pretty well together sharing some things and having some special toys as well. It is a joy to see how much they love each other and treasure one another's company.

Story: Candles Light the Way

One story that I found very touching was about a 12-year-old only child who had a new baby brother. She was feeling very left out and unloved and could not understand how her parents could still love her and love the new baby boy. The mom got out four candles and told her daughter that the candles represented each of them. The mom said the first candle represented her and as she lit it she said the flame represents my love. The second one, she said, represents your father. Then she lit the second candle with the first candle and said that when she married him they gave each other their love and now look at the love they shared. Then, she said, you were born, and she lit the third candle and said look how the love in the family grew. Then the new baby was born and she lit the fourth candle and said now look how much love there is in our family. This is a very visual example for kids that are having a feeling of dethronement. In fact, some families have added it to their weekly family meetings.

Story: My Mom is Marrying Your Dad!

Niko and Joe became step-brothers as teenagers, and learned to share the TV, video games, bathroom, chores, and friends. It has been fun to watch the process. They are really happy to have a brother. They call each other for help, or to ask for a ride, and introduce each other to their friends. They are very happy for this great gift and what a surprise to have a new "child" in the house at this age.

Story: Three in a Chair

Jacob was two years and three months when Amil was born. I found many ways to keep Jacob involved in helping with his new baby brother. Things would go pretty smoothly until it was time to nurse the new baby. Jacob definitely felt a little left out. I quickly realized that there was certainly room in the chair or on the couch for Jacob to tuck in close to me and I could snuggle with him too. One day he had his favorite book with him and he simply opened it, turned the pages, and I read to him. Nursing suddenly became a wonderful family time for the three of us once we began reading stories together.

TIPS:

1. Offer Genuine Encounter Moments (GEMS) every day.

2. Allow older sibling to safely express both negative and positive feelings.

3. Have them help with the baby in age appropriate ways.

4. Have them teach the new sibling something.

5. Breathe.

6. Have fun.

Myth Twelve:
We Should Praise Our Children Often.

I realize there are books and experts out there telling you to constantly praise your kids, in fact to become their biggest cheerleader in order to motivate them to be the 'best' they can be. With this type of parenting you will be raising kids that are either 'pleasers' or ones that develop the attitude: "what's in it for me!" They will constantly look outside of themselves for approval (external motivation).

It seems so innocent in the beginning when we begin to reward our kids for using the toilet, then it moves on to rewards for staying in bed all night. We then move on to rewards for good grades or good behavior. Then age 16 comes along and they want a car for a reward for good grades. What if you cannot afford a car?

Yes, I know some of you reading this are saying, but it works! It works but the motivation to do it is the rewards (external) instead of the desire to do it because they want to (internal). A good question to ask yourself if you are a believer of this myth is: Who is going to be their cheerleader when they are adults? They will still be looking outside themselves for recognition and praise! For example, one of my recent graduates told me that in the business he owns he feels more like a cheerleader than the owner of a company. He spends the majority of his day patting backs and making sure everyone is feeling okay (external motivation) rather than being able to get the work done that is necessary to keep the business on track. He finds this very stressful, but also a great lesson he keeps using in order to help his children learn internal rather than external motivation.

New Idea:
Encouragement Helps Develop Internal Motivation in Kids

Teaching Point:

Ways to help develop internal motivation:

1. When your child gets an A or an award, instead of saying how proud you are or what a good child he is, say, "Congratulations, what do you think you did to get that A?" We want them to recognize what they did to be successful.

2. Talk to your child more like a friend rather than a child. You would never tell your friend what a good helper they were in the kitchen. You would simply thank them for helping.

3. Ask how they felt they did at school verses having them tell you what the teacher said about them.

4. Allow your kids just to be and not comment on every step they take.

5. When your child says, "Are you proud of me?" say, "First let me check in with you, how do you feel

about this?"

6. Be specific and honest with them when acknowledging their help.

Story: Goalie

Niko played goalie for the youth soccer league, and it became evident there how valuable encouragement is. A goalie can block many shots in one game, while the forward who scores one goal might get much more attention. And while Niko would block many shots, the one or two that made it in the goal could make all the difference in the game.

After the game, using encouraging phrases to let Niko share his feelings and his opinion of the game maintained our closeness. Rather than saying, "great job", or some other evaluative statement, I would either acknowledge Niko's emotion, such as "You look really happy/frustrated!", or a statement that was not evaluating his performance, such as "Wow, there was a lot of action on goal today!" By refraining from praise, which is evaluative, it kept the door open for communication and connection, whether the team won or lost.

Walton Story by Luke

I remember many times in my life when I was supported by my family. One of the more recent memories is draft day for the National Basketball Association (NBA). This was definitely one of the most nervous days of my life because

I did not know what team I might be drafted on or worse, whether I would even get drafted.

I had just been on the road for two months playing basketball hard almost every day trying out for different teams around the country. I was at my dad's house with all of my brothers. As we were watching the draft on TV, I was very nervous and I could see in my brothers' faces that they were both excited and nervous at the same time. As we watched them calling out the names for the draft, I did not say a word. My brothers nervously made some comments.

Finally, after what seemed like a very long time, when the Lakers called my name, all my brothers jumped all over me congratulating me and cheering for me. I mean, they did not even wait for them to say my whole name, just when they called out 'Luke' they were already jumping up with excitement for me. Later when my dad congratulated me, with tears in his eyes, I could see in his face that he was very proud of me too. It was really special for me to share this great moment with my family.

Walton Story by Susie

One time my nephew came over with his mom and excitedly informed me that he was student of the month. Jordin, age seven, waited for my praise to tell him how proud I was of him like most of the other adults had, but I didn't. Instead

I said, "Jordin, what did you do to get this award?" He looked at me and said, "I don't know." So I said, "Let's talk about it. Do you listen in class?" He said, "Yes." I said, "Do you cooperate?" He said "yes." "Do you hand in your homework packets on time?" He said, "Yes." I said, "Do you think those are some of the things you did to get the award?" He said, "Yes." I said, "Congratulations." He said, "Thanks Auntie" and he was just as happy then as when he first walked in, but he had more of a sense of what got him that award. That is what we are looking for, that internal motivation versus external.

You might say that external motivation is what makes the world go around. Trust me, your kids will still get all the awards and all the bonuses they need when they are internally motivated versus externally motivated.

Story: My Nephew by Susie

I have a nephew who is working in an investment firm and he never graduated from college. He got hired on as a temporary. He is so internally motivated that he's had about five promotions and they love him. It is not about a degree, it is about his motivation and his passion for what he does. So, let's get that going in your child and they'll have a much healthier adult life.

Walton Story: Newspaper Excerpts about Nathan

Nate4Gov? Why not? Nate Walton led Princeton to the 2001 Ivy basketball title. Now, at age 25, he wants to lead California. Doesn't matter who you are: Professor, Teammate, Coach, Reporter. When Nate Walton speaks, your natural inclination is to listen. Some people are like that. They lead. Others follow them. It's like Pete Carril used to say: You can't separate the person from the player. Nate Walton lives like he played basketball at Princeton. His walk is confident and assured without any fake bravado. Same with his speech. He is funny and loose all the time, yet he knows exactly when it's time to become deadly serious. He is, for lack of a better way of putting it, the personification of California Cool. And once you understand all of that, you come to the same conclusion he did: Why not Nate Walton?

Nate Walton, Class of 2001, can be found in two places this fall: the Stanford Business School and the ballot for governor of California. "Princeton was the greatest place for me," Nate says. "It's inspired me to try to do great things in my life." Nate has been pointed in the direction of activism and public service his entire life. Both of his parents - his mother Susie and his father Bill, the Hall of Fame basketball player, who divorced when he was young - have stressed to him the importance of addressing the larger issues in society. Nate has taken the Princeton motto "in the nation's service" quite literally.

Nate had been working in New York City with a human rights group while waiting to start work on his MBA at Stanford. He was home for the summer relaxing on the night that Arnold Schwarzenegger announced on Jay Leno's show that he was going to run for governor as part of the Gray Davis recall vote. "I figured if Arnold could run so could I."

To be on the ballot, a candidate needed to secure 65 signatures of registered voters and pay a $3,500 fee (or, to avoid the fee, get at least 10,000 signatures). Nate's father promised to pay the fee, and the 25-year-old would-be governor set out to collect the signatures. "It was easy," he says. Don't be fooled into thinking that this is all a joke to him. While he is not actively campaigning all day until the Oct. 7 election, he has done many television, radio and newspaper interviews. He has good name recognition through his father, arguably the greatest college basketball player of all-time, and his brother Luke, who plays for the Los Angeles Lakers. Once the cameras and microphones are turned on, Nate Walton can more than hold his own. Unlike many of the candidates in this election, Nate is extremely well-versed on the issues facing California, and he never flinches when asked for a position.

Nate is just beginning his graduate work at Stanford. "The people here think it's interesting," he says of his new classmates. "For me, it's been overwhelmingly about talking to people about issues. And when he's a little more settled?

Is this the start of a career in politics? "I'm not sure," he says. "Let's call it an experiment. I'm going to vote 'no' on the recall. To me, that's not the way to go about democracy. At the same time, this has been too good an opportunity for me. And it's been a lot of fun, getting out and talking to people."

TIPS:

1. When your child has a success today, instead of saying anything, remain silent and just watch the joy in his or her face.
2. Say thank you instead of good boy or good job when they are being helpful.
3. Ask them what they think or feel about a success instead of responding with praise.
4. Inspire your kids to do what they are passionate about.
5. Breathe, and as always, Have Fun!

Myth Thirteen:
Mistakes are Bad.

We are human beings and we are not perfect, so mistakes will always be made. If we live with the belief that mistakes are bad, we will definitely travel a rough road! For many of us this idea gets driven home at the start of going to school when we receive the big red check mark for each misspelled word or when we spill our milk at home and get scolded for filling the glass too high or being careless. How freeing and enriching it is when we learn that mistakes are Great Teachable Moments! The more mistakes you make in life the smarter you become!!

New Idea:
Mistakes are Wonderful Opportunities to Learn.

Story: Breakfast of Champion Story

At three-years-old, Garret was not only capable, but insisted on getting his own breakfast. If he spilled his milk, cereal or orange juice he would grab a dishtowel and clean it up while singing, "A mistake is a great opportunity to learn. I care enough to repair my mistake!!"

Walton Story About Luke

In an interview in the San Diego Union Tribune, Luke and coach Phil Jackson were asked about some mistakes the team had made throughout the year. Luke said: "You learn a lot more from actually making the mistakes than from someone telling you. It is like that in all aspects of life. Your parents can tell you everything, but until you experience that mistake, that's when you really learn from it."

Teaching Point:

The more mistakes your kids make living with you, the less you will worry about them when they are older. Think of a mistake as a wonderful opportunity to learn. Turn your mistakes into teachable moments not punishing moments. This is an important one to remember. Mistakes are not bad. They are experiences. Some kids are going to need to make mistakes in order to learn.

Society sees mistakes as failure. We were brought up like that in most classrooms. You have a test of fifteen spelling words and you miss four and the teacher puts big red marks next to the four you missed. There is no celebration of the eleven words you got correct.

We are always looking for perfection. We wonder why our kids have such a hard time when they make mistakes. When we become afraid of making mistakes we are limiting ourselves to the full experience of life. I invite you to begin looking at mistakes as a wonderful opportunity to learn.

Story: Jonas Salk

Someone once asked Jonas Salk how he felt when he had so many different failures before he found the polio vaccine? What kept him going mistake after mistake? He responded that in his family when they made a mistake it was never thought of as a failure, but as another experience. He got so much joy and so much information in those "so called" mistakes than had he found the vaccine right off the bat.

Story: Teenage Dilemma

I have a friend who is a father to three daughters. When they made mistakes, he didn't punish them. When things calmed down, he would sit them down and they would talk about how they could do things differently if it was to come up again. When these girls were teenagers they'd often say to their dad, "Dad, why can't you just be a normal dad and yell at us or ground us, or send us to our room. Why do we always have to talk about these mistakes?" He said to them, "Is there a better time to learn?"

Teaching Point:

As parents we can quit beating ourselves and our kids up when they make mistakes and say, "Okay, what a great time to learn." For some kids, making mistakes is how they learn. Let's not look at it as a negative thing, let's think of it as a time of growth. You want your kids to make their mistakes when they are living at home and they have you to help them through it. You don't want a child who never admits to making a mistake because when they go out into the world, they probably will make mistakes and you will not be there to help them sort it out. So, let them make mistakes, grow from their mistakes and learn from their mistakes, and not shame and blame them. Let's celebrate mistakes as an opportunity to learn.

When your child makes a mistake instead of reacting out of anger or frustration, take a step back, and pause for a moment, take a deep breath. A pause can be two seconds, two minutes, or 20 minutes, depending on how upset you are, and then look at the situation and ask, "What is my intention here? Is it to create closeness or distance?" If you want to create distance with your child in that moment, you will do your yelling or screaming. If you want to create closeness, take a deep breath and say, "Okay the milk is spilled, what needs to be done?" Or you might just walk over to the sink and get the sponge and a bottle of non-toxic counter spray and hand it to your child and without any words let him know it's time to clean up. Then, you can ask, after taking time to clean things up, "What can you do differently next time you want some milk?" You can brainstorm with your child.

Story: The Bicycle Make Up

When my oldest son was about 12-years-old, he went out riding his bicycle in the neighborhood. After quite a while, we went to call him in and couldn't find him. We called our family who lived close by and several of us went around the neighborhood looking for him. When we did find him, instead of yelling at him and pushing him away, we sat him down and told him how scared we were and how we needed him to communicate with us when he's going to be somewhere else.

Then we talked to him about how so many of us were looking for him and how because he hadn't communicated many people were inconvenienced and then we asked him what he wanted to do about that. He decided to do a make-up for every person. He helped me get dinner ready, helped his Poppa with the yard work the next day, helped his Nana with her dog and helped his dad by watching his little sister while he finished a project. In the end, not only had he remedied his mistake but he also got to spend some one-on-one time with everyone and was able to get closer to those people who love him.

<u>Story: Let the Mistake do the Talking...not You....</u>

At age two, Garret was independent and curious. He put an entire roll of toilet paper in the toilet one day. Instead of getting angry and saying, that's a "no, no," I stood and watched his amazement as he flushed the toilet to see what would happen. We fished the drenched roll from the toilet as he told me, "Only a little bit works mommy." He never did it again.

Story: Letting Go of the Idea of What is Right

My five-year-old son Marino loves to cook with me, but he has a hard time accepting that to get the results we want, we have to follow a plan and a recipe. His impulse is to just combine whatever ingredients come to his mind, and he sometimes wants to include exotic ingredients like weeds, stones, or dirt.

A few months ago, he wanted to make cookies -- but he was determined to make up his own recipe. At first, I tried to tell him we had to follow a recipe or the cookies wouldn't come out right -- then I thought, what would it cost me to let him learn that for himself? A bit of flour and sugar, an egg, some salt, oregano (his recipe!) -- we might not have cookies we wanted to eat, oh well! So I let him lead the process -- we made the cookies according to his recipe -- and before we even finished mixing the dough, he was ready to do something else. That's when I realized cooking for him wasn't necessarily about the results.

Last week Marino really wanted to help me make pizza. I had the dough ready on the counter and the ingredients ready to assemble (including capers, his suggestion). He got to the kitchen before me, and when I came in he had stuck a couple of sticks into the dough. At first I felt tense and wondered if this was such a good idea -- and I started to give him a lecture on following the rules for making pizza. His lip got a bit pouty and I could sense this was turning into a power struggle -- not what I wanted.

I remembered the cookie dough incident and how cooking for him was about being creative and exploring. I saw there was plenty of dough, so I pulled off a chunk for him to make his own pizza while I made one for the family. He was so happy rolling out a pizza snake on his tray, and decorating it with a bit of sauce, shredded mozzarella, and capers -- I doubted it would taste very good, but I'm proud to say I kept my mouth shut. He also helped put toppings on the big pizza and we put them both in the oven.

When we served them up, he was really excited about his artistic pizza -- until he bit into it and realized it was pretty dry and mostly doughy. After a couple bites, he asked if he could have a piece of our pizza, and I said sure. We left it at that -- and instead of him feeling like he had to rebel against my rules, he discovered something about cooking for himself, and we had a wonderful time together.

TIPS:

1. Teach children to repair mistakes (your example is key in this).
2. Set up a cleaning supply area at your children's level.
3. Sit down after a mistake is made and talk about how to do it differently next time.
4. Treat a mistake as a great opportunity to learn.
5. Breathe.
6. Have fun.

Myth Fourteen:
Traumatic Events Scar
Children for Life.

Traumatic events can scar a child for life if that is your belief or they can be used as a way to build resiliency and inner strength. It will mainly depend on how the adults handle the situation. We are our child's lifeline to the universe. If we are okay... they will be okay. It is not about minimizing the event, but more about how to use it as a way to bring the family closer together. We all agree how horrible 9/11 was when it happened. And do you remember how loving and caring people became afterwards? There were less people honking at each other, and more people allowing a car to get in front of them while driving. It made us realize as a country how valuable life is and not to sweat the small stuff. It was finding the gift in that experience and that is what we are talking about here.

New Idea:
When Dealt with Properly,
Traumatic Events Build Resiliency.

Each difficult event that happens in our lives can be utilized for growth and to build resilience. Resilience is taught, often through challenging situations. It does not mean one lives life in a survivor mode or in a fear mode. It means you go through the bumps in life using each situation to make you stronger. At each situation, you have a choice to move closer to life or to step away. Learning to accept what is happening, to move closer to life, and learning from difficult situations is called resilience. It helps us to honor the life we have.

Story: A 9/11 Tragedy

That day was Mikki's (our four-year-old's) first day of school. My husband, Don and I had made such a big thing out of going to school that I felt I could do no less then take her to school at 1PM. I picked Mikki up from the babysitter and took her to her first day of school. She was so excited. When we arrived at the door of her classroom I looked at the teacher and told her I needed the minister immediately. He saw me right away and I told him what I thought might be happening in our lives and I wanted to make sure that what I told Mikki would not be detrimental. I told him that I was not going to say anything to her until she asked and then I wanted to tell her the truth and that her father was now one of her guardian angels. He absolutely agreed and said he would always be there to help and he was.

Mikki asked nothing the first night. The morning of the 12th she looked at me and asked where daddy was. I told her that he was next to her as her guardian angel now and would always be there. I explained that we would no longer be able to see him with our outer eyes but we could with our inner eyes. She understood immediately and then asked what happened. I explained that some very bad men had flown a plane into daddy's building and now daddy was home with God. That answer satisfied her and it opened the door for us to always be able to talk about him, which we did and still do. I never allowed her to see anything on TV related to 9/11 and I kept her routine as normal as I could. Normal routines made sense and it helped both of us keep Don alive in our hearts. I had a wonderful babysitter who helped me with this!

As Mikki grew older the questions changed, as did the answers. I always told the truth in a way she could understand. I never made anything up. Mikki's responses also changed. As she grew older and asked questions she had an increased level of sadness. When she realized, at about nine-years-old, that she was not the only one who lost her dad she was very sad and shocked. Mikki went to a 9/11/01 camp for the first time last year and when she arrived home she said it was the first time she felt whole. She was in a group of nine girls all of whom lost their dads that day. Mikki is a compassionate, loving and wise eleven-year-old now who loves life, her family, and friends.

Story: Lily's Mom

It was Labor Day just after my daughter Lily's second birthday, when my wife of nine years got sick. She was diagnosed with stage three cervical cancer. At the time I was self-employed (owned a construction company) and we had Lily, whom we had adopted at birth. We were actually beginning the paperwork to adopt another child. Our life changed drastically, fast. It was surgeries, hospitals, chemo, and radiation. All of this proved to be very challenging for me. Gina was so sick, I took on the parenting role completely. I would also have to try and keep Lily at a distance from Gina due to the fact she was in so much pain. It was too much for her to handle a rambunctious two-year-old. As far as my parenting skills where concerned during that period of time, they were not on track to raise a well-adjusted child. I was in survival mode. I loved and care for my daughter more then anything, I just did not have the experience or know how to create a healthy environment. I really did not have a structured schedule for her, and I can see how that led to more chaos. Due to the stress I was under, I would give in to Lily on almost everything. She did not have a bedtime and she slept in our bed. I did not have her sit down and eat on a schedule and was constantly making her meals and snacks.

Gina died at home in my arms two weeks after Lily's third birthday. The day she passed away Lily was with her aunt (Gina's sister). I brought Lily back home that evening and she ran through the house looking for Gina and then she asked me where's mommy. I was at a loss. In the best way I could, I explained that mommy was watching over us and when you talk to her she can hear you. I had told Gina before she passed that I would tell Lily to look at the moon and she could talk to her. So I told Lily that she could look at the moon and talk and mom would be looking at the same time. To this day she still talks to the moon. At Christmas time, she wrote a card to her mommy and asked me if we could send it to her. I thought for a moment and then told her we could. We went to the party store and got a helium-filled balloon. We then went down to the beach, tied the card to the balloon and Lily let it go. She likes having a way to connect with her mom.

Story: A Different Story

I was married for 35 years to a wonderful man who was a post-polio quadriplegic. We were blessed with two sons but I have to admit, I was a little concerned about what life would be like for two boys with a father that could not run and play with them. My husband was wonderful with the children but I did notice some feelings in the boys when they began to go to school and participate in sports. They saw that their father was different. When they shared this with me, I tried to listen without judging them. In no way, however, did this difference interfere in creating a very deep relationship between father and sons; perhaps it even made it deeper. They loved to play music together, discuss matters together, work on computers together, and go places together. The boys also learned an incredible compassion for all people, particularly those who have disabilities, while still being able to see them as whole people with so many gifts to share. As young married men, both my boys show a commitment, sensitivity, and love to their families and to all they come in contact with.

Story: Okay, Son, We're in For a Rough Ride, Hold On Tight!

When my husband, after 18 years together, unexpectedly decided to end our marriage, my son and I were shocked and dismayed. We cried together and cocooned at home together. We pulled together as a team to sell our home, pack our belongings, reduce our living expenses, and start a new life together.

I was blessed to understand the grieving process, and I knew that we would experience pain and that we would get through it and be fine. We didn't choose what was happening, but we could choose to accept it and to actively participate in the healing process. I explained the grieving process to him: denial, anger, bargaining, depression, and acceptance. I told him that we would have lots of different feelings, like sadness, anger, and wishing things were different. I let him know that if I was crying, it was OK, it was healthy to let it out, and he didn't have to worry about me, and he didn't have to do anything to fix it or to take care of me. Most of all, I let him know that we were going to be fine, just like when he broke his arm and it hurt a lot, and he couldn't play sports for a while, but then it healed and it was good as new. We decided to honor a traditional one-year mourning period, and at the end of the year, we made it a point to have a lot of fun so that my son would see the full cycle of loss and recovery/moving on.

Now, three years after my divorce, I am engaged to be married to a wonderful man. My son is happy and well-adjusted, and is prepared to handle the ups and downs of life. He wrote in his senior reflection paper, "The divorce taught me how to support people in their time of need and has taught me how to recover from hard times in life."

Story: A Sign of Self Reliance is to Know How to Ask For Help

Elizabeth was just a toddler when she was run over by our family car in a tragic turn of events at home. Her jaw was broken and had to be replaced. Because she was so young, she would have multiple surgeries throughout her childhood to replace the bone as she grew. Each surgery required a hospital stay, and then recovery at home with her jaw wired shut, missing school and friends. I learned to make her favorite soups and to puree the soup to a thin consistency. She learned to ask for help and to allow others to care for her, as well as to be independent and resilient. As a young adult she has found the lessons she learned as a child to be very helpful.

Walton Story by Susie

I come from a very close and loving family of ten children. When I was 11 my little seven-year-old sister, Cindy, died just before Christmas and we were all devastated. My mom was particularly bereft, since she loved each of her children so dearly. At this point Mom said she felt like she had two choices, lose herself in sorrow and alcohol or turn to faith in God - she chose to get ever closer to God. What my dad learned from this sad event was the importance of becoming less autocratic and more playful. He began to realize on a deeper level how precious life is. So the death of my little sister actually brought us even closer together as a family. We do not get as caught up in pettiness or difference because we learned how valuable life is from my mom and dad.

Nine years later in 1971, my Dad died of a heart attack. He was only 56 years old, not over weight and fairly athletic. It was a tremendous shock. Once again, the hardest hit was my Mom. She and Dad had been sweethearts since she was 16. But once again, she helped us create even more closeness in our family because she modeled such love and faith during this very difficult time. She still had three children in high school and grammar school and so she forged ahead with life and keeping the family going.

After three years, she decided to move to Maui, Hawaii with the remaining children. This was the place that she and Dad had dreamed about moving to after my Dad retired. My Mom was always the master at living out her dreams.

After many years of marriage and having four sons together, my husband and I divorced in 1989. I felt it was so important to show the sadness of the situation and at the same time to move forward in my life. I had learned resilience from my parents, watching them deal with hard turns in life. I knew I also wanted to model to my children how change, even when it is sad and difficult, can be positive and how it can build resilience.

When my sister, grandma (my mom's mother, who lived with us) and my dad, all died within a ten year span, the gift our family received was closeness and resilience. My mom was amazing to watch through these difficult times. Of course she was deeply saddened by each of these events, but she never stopped looking forward. She has always been such an inspiration to me. My mother was a living example of the words...

Dance as though no one is watching you -
Love as though you've never been hurt before -
Sing as though no one can hear you -
Live as though heaven is on earth ....
Unknown

In 1999, my mom died at the age of 81 of cancer at her home in Maui. What an incredibly loving and resilient woman my mom was. I miss her so much. And I feel she has passed that on to all of her children and grandchildren. I watch my sons and I see the resilience in each of them.

Adam Devadatta, my oldest son, was born three weeks early and weighed five pounds. He had no sucking reflex for the first day so I spoon-fed him my breast milk until he was able to breast feed. At six weeks old, when he was a whopping six pounds, we went to Maui for two months and stayed with my mom and brother. In two months the combination of sunshine, warm ocean breezes (he took many naps outside in his buggy under palm trees), and lots of love, he gained six pounds and has never looked back. His first passage to resilience.

In fourth grade he was at a friend's house and got locked out of the friend's house and was stuck in the back yard with a pretty aggressive dog. He was scared to death, but instead of creating a fear of dogs, he has developed an unbelievable love for animals, especially dogs.

Adam has always walked to the beat of his own drum. He is a teacher to the rest of us in our family. He grew up in a basketball family. When we lived in Boston he loved going to Celtic practices and watching players like his dad, Kevin

McHale, Scott Wedman, and Larry Bird playing basketball while having fun. Adam learned to play with this love. He was beautiful to watch on the court - he almost always had a smile on his face. The thing is, Adam doesn't have a bit of competition in him and this would drive his high school and college coaches crazy. How could a kid with such potential not have the drive to be the best?

Little did these coaches know that Adam was there to give them the gift of seeing someone playing for the pure joy of the sport. Sure he wanted to win, but more importantly he wanted them to see him for who he was, not who he wasn't.

Adam went through some very difficult times transitioning out of playing basketball. But he has never lost the joy of the game and I feel it has allowed him to take a closer look at his gift and not get caught up in performance and competition. He is a true team player in every part of his life. In fact, I don't think I have ever heard him speak negatively about anyone. As we say in our family, our team, he is the voice of reason. When he speaks he speaks truth.

My second son, Nathan Whitecloud, is one of my Indigo (self reliant, headstrong, creative, and intuitive) children. In most families there is usually one child who is the barometer of the family. On our team, that would be Nathan. Where Adam breathes serenity, Nathan breathes life. Nathan's life is based on resilience. I used to tell him if he made it to age six he would make it to 106. Well, he is 30 and going strong.

From the time Nathan was six months old until he was ten he had bronchial pneumonia three times a year. Talk about building resilience. With the help of a homeopath and other alternative medicines, he was able to build up the resilience to fight his illnesses and is now as strong as an ox.

As Adam experienced, Nathan got to spend his formative years watching the Celtics and learning how to play team ball while having fun. Nathan has an incredible drive and he is one that needs to experience as much as he possibly can. He has such an internal drive, along with a belief system that he can accomplish anything he puts his mind to. As a result, he had a very successful high school experience playing basketball.

As a junior at Princeton University, he had surgery on his ankle, but that did not stop him from playing basketball. In his senior year he became one of the leading all-time assist persons. Princeton also won the Ivy League title that year, which few people thought possible. But the internal maturation and passion which team-captain Nathan brought to the team that year did wonders for the team and its play. When it comes to our family, Nathan is the one you can count on to remember our birthdays and check in to see how everyone is doing. He is the heartbeat, which is essential in any team.

My third son is Luke Theodore. When Luke was born the first words spoken to him were from the midwife, who said, "Welcome to the world angel of God." I have to say that blessing has stayed with him. Luke was born with an innate sense of knowing who he is and an amazing depth of love.

His growth in resilience was in education. In first grade the teacher noticed Luke wasn't learning to read. We had him tested and found out he had an auditory learning disability. Fortunately, we had support from his teacher at St. Vincent and I was able to take him three mornings a week to a tutor who taught him to read through the Lindamood-Bell Learning System. It is actually a way all kids can learn to read, but for some reason most schools push the phonetic way of teaching reading.

Luke is an extremely visual learner, so with the help of teachers like Linda Colby he learned to compensate for his weakness with the strengths he had. He took this very seriously and excelled.

Luke did very well in school and graduated from the University of Arizona with a degree in Family Studies. He also played basketball under the tutelage of Hall of Fame Coach, Lute Olson. When Luke was being recruited by Arizona, he took a trip to the campus where he met the team, along with the Coach and his late wife, Bobbi. When he got home from the weekend he told me that was where he wanted to go to school. When I asked him why, he said that the team felt like a family and Mrs. Olson (Bobbi), was a lot like me and he knew it was where he wanted to be. He loved it there.

As you can see, family comes in all descriptions. As I mentioned earlier, Luke graduated with a degree in Family Studies. My mom, who also was a graduate of University of Arizona had a degree in Home Economics, was diagnosed with cancer during Luke's freshman year and passed away before he declared his major. What we didn't realize at the time was that they had the same degrees. Family Studies was once known as Home Economics, which made the degree even more meaningful.

Luke is now playing basketball with the Los Angeles Lakers. His rookie season, he was able to play along side Shaq, Kobe, and Karl Malone just to name a few, and was coached by Phil Jackson. It was an incredible experience for him. What an environment for a first year player. He is now in his sixth year and through ups and down his resilience has grown and he has learned more than ever to believe in himself.

My youngest son, Christopher William was born, like his brother, Adam on Halloween. We had just moved to Menlo Park, California, a couple of weeks before. Adam was having his birthday party and I started to go into labor. All four boys were born at home, so I was hoping to get through the birthday party before Christopher was born. But, I didn't.

There was Adam and his friends along with his dad celebrating his sixth birthday and I was in the bedroom with the midwives, my friend Karen, Luke, and Nathan, delivering Christopher. All the kids went home after the party and told their parents that Adam got a baby brother for his birthday. Three hours later it was costumes and trick-or-treat time, quite a full day. Christopher was a gift. I feel Christopher's resiliency comes from being the youngest of four incredibly strong-willed kids, not to mention parents. He learned at a young age to stand up for himself and I must say he is incredibly self-reliant which he learned by having to be his own person from the get go.

When Christopher graduated he had hopes of playing professional basketball but his body had a different idea and so it is. He is not playing but has taken what he has learned in life and is busy making things happen.

TIPS:

1. Model healthy care for yourself during difficult times.

2. Allow kids to have and express their feelings.

3. Encourage them without rescuing them.

4. Let them know you are there to support them.

5. Let them know you have feelings.

6. Remember to have fun.

Myth Fifteen:
It's My Job to Keep My Children Happy and to Protect Them From Getting Hurt.

You may be thinking, life is scary or dangerous, but my question to you is do you want your children living in fear or do you want them living in awareness? There is no better teacher than life itself. Yes, of course, as parents we want to protect our children from the downs in life but what if you change your belief and start allowing your kids to experience more of life?

New Idea:
Allow Natural or Logical Consequences To Happen.

What will happen if I don't intervene? If it is nothing that causes physical harm or humiliation, then let it happen! That is a natural consequence, and they are the best teachers in life. Usually, they come about when we do not expect them, such as a child climbing on a park bench who happens to slip and fall. Sometimes as a parent, you can set up natural consequences. As an example, you are at the beach and you told your child not to get close to the water as a wave could knock her down, but she persists anyway. You are standing right next to her. Stop warning her and let the wave knock her down. In other words, let the wave do the teaching, not you.

Story: Learning about the Consequence of Stealing

When my son was six-years-old a friend of his showed him the ropes for shoplifting candy at the local candy store. My son put some candy in his pocket and got caught. The store called the police. Meanwhile, I drove past the store and saw my son being questioned by the police. I wanted to stop and protect my son but I knew it was the best lesson he could learn, that the consequence of shoplifting is getting in trouble with the law.

Story: Monkey Bars

Hailey, my five year old, wanted to cross some monkey bars and I told her that I thought they were way too far apart and way too high off the ground for her. She insisted that they weren't. I wanted to tell her that she couldn't because "she would get hurt." Instead I thought to myself "what is the worst that could happen?" I decided that there was a chance she could fall and maybe even get hurt, but the chances were slim that she would die or break a bone. So I decided not to stop her.

I watched her climb the ladder and then contemplate going across. I walked closer to her and let her know that I would be right here if she wanted to call on me but unless she asked for my help, I would not interfere. She started across and right away found that her arms were not long enough to reach the next bar. I did not make a move. (So hard!!) She hung for a moment and finally dropped, slightly twisting her ankle.

She looked up at me and started to cry and I asked her what she felt she needed right now. To my surprise, she said she wanted to try again but this time she wanted me to stand underneath her in case she wanted me to catch her. That time she was able to hang a little longer and had a lot of confidence in doing so. She dropped and this time did not get hurt. I know that by letting her have her own experience, she learned how to problem-solve and ask for help when she needed it. And it helped me to see that by allowing her to take a chance, I allowed her to grow.

Story: Ally Learns to Swim

My favorite story about shifting the paradigm of "Life is Dangerous" or that I must protect my child from ever getting hurt (as though I could do that, right?) is of Ally wanting to learn to swim at age three. Ally is an only child and came into this world under very Divine and collaborative circumstances. Those circumstances created a princess which would make it easy as a parent to take on the "I must protect my child" attitude. But, if you want to raise a self-reliant child who has the confidence to get what they want out of life, you cannot create the belief "life is dangerous", or they must be protected.

The summer of Ally's third year our family was swimming at the condominium pool. Ally and I were floating on noodles and dog paddling across the pool from the steps to the ladder on the opposite side. Ally would look around every four feet or so with a big old smile on her face that said, "look at me - I'm swimming." Of course this was all encouraged by the adults in the pool and sitting on the side and responding back with things like "isn't she sweet," "yes, you are swimming," "you're so brave." And, on and on they went - inspiring the princess of the pool.

Well, as we returned to the steps to take a break from our dog paddling a woman walked down the steps - dipped into the water - and proceeded to swim the breast stroke across the pool. Ally, observing her, said " I want to swim like that." My heart sank! I was just about to tell her that she wasn't old enough to swim and that she couldn't do it when I realized that to tell her this would be incredibly discouraging to her. It would send the message that she wasn't capable. It would send the message that she wasn't strong enough. Most of all - it would send the message that I didn't believe in her. I had no idea what to do, but I knew in that moment I was committing to stop myself from sending any of these possible messages to her. All of these possible messages were my beliefs about life: not hers and they are not the beliefs and values I wanted to instill in her. I want Ally to be confident, capable and most of all I want her to know EVERY day and

EVERY minute how much I DO believe in her. So – you guessed it. I proceeded to stand by VERY, VERY closely and let natural consequences take their due process. Ally stepped off into the swimming pool doing the breast stroke with her arms as quickly as she could.......and......proceeded to sink. Yes, her head went under, she began to kick and struggle and as she did I caught her very lovingly and picked her up giving her a big hug and telling her what a great job she did. She had just tried to do the breast stroke at three-years-old. That took confidence. Ally's response was "get me a towel. I need something to wipe my eyes." We walked to the side of the pool, got the towel and she dried her eyes. After she was done, we both began to laugh and giggle about her first swimming lesson.

We still tell the story. Ally still loves swimming. Most of all – Ally believes in all she does and has more confidence than most adults I know. Natural consequences have provided Ally the opportunity to make her own decisions about life and how she wants to live – not based on my consequences as a child, or an adult. For that I AM grateful.

Story: Consequences Help Children Take Responsibility

Our six-year-old daughter Mary had a hard time getting up and ready for school in the morning. Every morning was a struggle and ended with a frantic rush to get out the door for school. We finally put the responsibility on her. We bought her an alarm clock so she could get up on time. We told her we weren't going to tell her over and over to get ready for school every day. It was her responsibility to get up and get ready for school. If she was late, she would have to go to the office and explain why she was late. It was her responsibility to "own it." We followed through with our part, and she did as well. She hasn't been late for school since and the mornings are much more enjoyable.

Teaching Point:

When you are not willing to allow a natural consequence to occur then use a logical consequence. Logical consequences are not about teaching a lesson. A logical consequence is about setting a limit for acceptable behavior. Logical consequences work best when they come out of a mutual agreement you have made with your child. When setting a logical consequence, it is best to follow the format of the five "R's". The consequence must be respectful, reasonable, related, teach responsibility, and have a resolution.

Story: Bike Away

My child kept leaving his bike out in the front yard. Since I was not willing to have him experience the natural consequence (having his bike stolen), I knew I should work on a logical consequence. The first step was for me to own the problem (why don't I want my son to leave his bike in the front yard). I then sat down with my child and said: "I have a problem with you leaving your bike out in the front yard. I am afraid some one might take it." Then my son and I came to an agreement on how to handle the problem, which was that when he was done riding his bike, he would put it in the garage. I thanked him for working with me on my problem and then the two of us decided on what the consequence would be if he forgot to honor his agreement. My son first said, you can give my bike away if I do not put it away. I showed him the list of the five "R's" and let him know that giving his bike away is not reasonable. We eventually came up with the consequence that if I end up putting the bike away, it will stay away for 24 hours and then my son can try again.

Teaching Point:

As your kids become older, you will find less need to implement logical consequences as you will be working together to resolve conflicts through conflict resolution and win win agreements. For younger children, consequences are more effective when they are implemented as quickly as possible.

Story: Shop, Shop, Shop

My child usually wants to walk with me in the store versus being in the shopping cart. I tell her that you may either hold on to the shopping cart or the consequence will be that I will put you back in the cart. If she lets go of the cart, I do not warn her or threaten her, I just lovingly pick her up and put her back in the cart and say we can try again later.

TIPS:

1. Stop remembering for your child.
2. Let the consequence do the talking.
3. When setting a logical consequence own the problem.
4. Logical consequences work best when talked about first.
5. If something works for a while and then stops working, do not give up, just renegotiate and come up with a new idea.
6. Have fun.

Myth Sixteen:
Repeated Yelling at Children Seems to Be the Only Way to Get Things Done.

Many of us were raised in homes where yelling was a common occurrence. I for one was a 'yeller' purely out of frustration, wanting my boys to do what I had asked them to do. It seemed like they wouldn't listen until I yelled at them. In fact, I yelled so much they nicknamed me 'Brubaker'. For those who do not know this movie, he was a prison warden. I remember thinking there had to be a better way to get them to do their chores. You don't need to yell at a dog to sit. Why was it that I needed to yell at my sons? Oh, and by the way, it did not promote cooperation. What it did was invite more yelling and complaining from them!

The whole notion that we must break them down by yelling or punishing, in order to build them up, especially with our strong-willed children, is not going to cut it any longer. I can tell you from my own personal experience as a teen this did not work. It only made me want to be even more defiant with my swim coach and certain teachers. I was so busy proving they couldn't MAKE me do what they wanted me to do that I missed out on a lot of opportunities.

Walton Story by Susie

My swim coach called my mom and told her she should have

---

a word with me and take away a privilege because he felt that I wasn't giving my all during the workout and I was wasting her money. So I responded with "fine, I will just quit." That was not what my coach had in mind. He was hoping it would motivate me to swim faster. It took him two weeks to get me back in the water and as a result I lost two weeks of training, which was a lot for a serious swimmer.

New Idea:
Try Something New.

The following stories will give you some fun and easy ideas on how to create more cooperation with our kids.

Story: The Barking Mother

One morning instead of barking out orders I said to my daughter, "let's have some fun today. You know what you need to do to get ready on time. When it's time to leave I'll meet you in the car." In the meantime, she's playing with the dog and I'm bursting at the seams but don't say anything. She got herself out the door on time, even though she was playing with everything. It was a big lesson for me. She knows what she needs to do and it may not be perfect, but I didn't have to say one word to her.

She's doing really well since I quit barking at her. She's 10 and I really have seen a shift since I stopped barking out a thousand orders a day. Instead I ask, what do you need to do today? I can ask "What are your chores today?" and she writes them down and checks them off. Before when I only barked orders at her, it only brought resistance from her, so it's a big change for us.

Story: Bedtime Word

Kate is three-years-old and its time for bed. She did not want to go to bed, but she already had pj's on and had taken her bath. I said the word bed and lovingly guided her back to bed. She got in then started complaining that no one wanted to sleep with her. I started talking with her a little (not good). She stayed in her room but I heard her up and playing about five minutes later. I did the guiding back into bed only this time I said "bedtime" with no eye contact. She got in bed and then 20 minutes later came out again. I got up and started guiding her again and said "bedtime." Then she stiff bodied me. I kept saying bedtime and I rubbed her back or her arms and started guiding her again. She would walk a little and then stiff body me again. I did the same as before, when I was close to her bed I picked her up and put her in bed. I stayed and rubbed her back a little, probably two minutes, then she stayed in bed for the rest of the night.

Story: The Nose Signal

My wife and I struggle with our youngest daughter at mealtime trying to get her to eat over her plate. After she's done, there is a huge circle of food around her chair. We guessed by four she'd be over it, but it's still an issue. We decided to try an alternative solution because repeating "Kimberly, please eat over your plate" wasn't getting through. I think she was as tired of hearing it as we were of saying it. Our solution was to teach her that when we point at our nose, it means "eat over your plate." That simple solution has already paid off immediately. As soon as we point to our nose, she smiles, sits up and eats over her plate. She even points to her nose and says "This means eat over my plate!" We're all having fun with it now and it adds some relief at mealtime for everyone.

Walton Story by Susie

Here's a story and an exercise my boys and I still do when we all get together.

Learning about Encouragement Feasts in the parenting class, "Redirecting Children's Behavior" by Kathryn Kvols, is what changed our family dynamics more than anything. During an encouragement feast you put one person in a circle and everyone tells that person what he or she loves about him or her, and then the next person goes in the circle until everyone gets to hear what others love about him or her. We all love each other, but how often do you tell someone what you really like about them. And it can be simple. When my boys first started doing it, they'd say things like, Nathan what I like about you is that you let me look at your baseball cards. What I like about you, mom is that you made me dinner last night. So you're not looking for something really deep here, you're looking for something the kids can compliment each other for. The reason we do that is because it teaches kids how to give compliments and it teaches kids how to take a compliment. It also makes it a lot more difficult to be mean or say a mean thing to someone you just received a compliment from.

It's a great way to create closeness and it is not just for families. I know people who do it at the start of a staff meeting. Normally, you would begin your family meeting with an encouragement feast, but it's something you can do throughout the week whenever you feel that there's a need. At times when the boys and I were getting grumpy, I'd say, "Okay, sounds like we can use an encouragement feast". It got to the point where all their friends learned about the encouragement feast too. If it was someone's birthday, we'd all give that one person an encouragement feast. When the boys' high school coach turned 40, I had 16 teenage boys telling their coach what they loved and respected about him. Often times when I was driving a bunch of kids to their basketball game I would have them turn to the person next to them in the car and share what they liked about their game. It's a very powerful exercise that you can use in any walk of life.

Story: Another Household Reports

One thing I do when my kids seem to be fighting with each other a lot is to start an encouragement feast. They both suggest this on their own at different times especially when I seem to be in a bad mood. It tends to alter the mood of the house and get us on the right track. They really love to have encouragement feasts and even like to compliment others who are not present, like their best friends and grandparents. Afterward the house seems to be calmer and we all get along better.

Story: Let's Have a Party

I was looking for ways to strengthen the relationship between my kids and me. I doubted that I could even create a close relationship with my two children. It seemed like I was always hurrying them around, yelling at them a lot, and never just being their friend. The next week I tried doing things a little different. Here is my story.

I took my two children, ages six and four to the doctor's for a checkup. It had been a busy day and after we finished and returned to the car, I began to start with what seemed to be an ongoing battle these days, yelling at the children to put on their seat belts before we could go. I decided to try something different then yelling at them. So we got in the car and I just sat there, sort of taking a break from the rushing, hectic day. Meanwhile, the children began talking and playing and having a good time. After awhile, they asked if they could have some of the treats I had bought earlier. It was only 4pm, not too close to dinner, so I decided to pull some out. We all sat there eating candy and talking. Suddenly my four-year-old son blurted out, "This is like a party!" After awhile the children put their seat belts on and we drove home.

At night, I usually go to bed early and get up at 5am before the children awake to get my chores done, and have a little time to myself. Two mornings after the car party, shortly after 5am, my four-year-old son came down the stairs with his little flashlight. I was so surprised to see him and at first a bit irritated because it was my time to get stuff done.

Then, remembering my parenting classes and looking at the bigger picture, I decided there were many mornings to get my work done and decided instead to take this time to be with my son. I asked why he was up so early. He said he wanted to have another party with me. I was more than a little shocked at his answer but asked him what a party would look like at this hour. He said, "parties always have ice cream", and that we should sit together and eat ice cream! I suggested we start with breakfast and then have ice cream for dessert. So I got some breakfast together and then decided to move a big chair up to the big living room window where we could sit together and snuggle as we ate our breakfast and watch the sky. First it was dark with only a few stars, and as we snuggled and ate, the sky slowly began to change colors until we saw the sun beginning to rise. It was so beautiful and snuggly, that we almost forgot the ice cream! It also was a wonderful experience with my son that I will always treasure.

Story: Using Signals Versus Words, Fun and Effective

I was having some problems with my three-year-old daughter Leslie. She seemed to whine whenever she wanted something. It really annoyed me and I allowed it to put me in a bad mood. I would be constantly asking her to say it differently and stop whining. Most of the time she would try to change her voice and ask in a nice way, but sometimes she refused and we would get into a battle. I would get angry and she would cry and neither of us got what we wanted.

Susie suggested that I try a signal with her. I told her that when she whined for things she wanted it really irritated me. I told her that when I pulled on my ear I wanted her to change the way she was talking to a polite way of speaking. She agreed and we went on with our day. The next time she started whining I just pulled on my ear and she changed the way she was talking immediately. It has worked ever since and we are both much happier.

Story: Children Want their Feelings Validated

My son, Dominic (almost five-years-old) asked if he could

begin working on a project (putting together a race track). I asked him to get dressed first and then we could do it together. He got angry and went into his room. He ripped off all the blankets, sheets, and pillows from his bed. In an effort NOT to create greater discord, I said casually, "Oh, I see you took off all of your covers, and that's okay because I needed to wash your sheets anyway." Dominic looked at me in frustration and stated clearly, " Mom, I ripped off the sheets because I was angry!"

I was trying to diffuse the situation by providing a light joke, or a "way out" for Dominic's behavior. But what he really needed was for me to say, "Wow you must be really mad." I learned from my mistake to be open and clear about what we're feeling.

Story: Edwin

Sometimes, when our daughter, Bea, will not cooperate or respond to requests to get dressed or to get into the car or bath, we call her by her favorite storybook cat's name, Edwin. One time when I was away on a trip with Bea, I was fit to be tied! None of my efforts to get Bea into PJs and start bedtime would work! I called my husband, partly to blow off steam, and told him what was going on - actually she was face down on the floor at the time, naked and not responding to a thing I said. My husband reminded me: "Did you try calling her Edwin?" I took his advice, said to Bea: "Edwin, kitty, kitty,

kitty, come here and let's get PJs on and read stories." Bea got up from the floor and cooperated with relative ease after what had been surely 15 minutes of non-cooperation.

I must add that she likes to be fed on the floor like a kitty at times. Thanks again for teaching us so much. I am sure Bea will thank you later!

Story: Learning a New Language!

We have a new language for our home. Phrases like "use your words," "how did that make you feel," "I am not willing to," and "how can you take care of yourself" have become a mainstay in how we parent. From enjoyable trips to the grocery store, to siblings who get along, to building self-esteem and self worth in our children what we have learned from Susie has given us a higher understanding of parenting.

I knew we had reached a point of success the other day when I was upset and my five-year-old Maddy said "Mom, what's wrong?" I said, "I don't want to talk about it" and she said "but Mom you have to talk about your feelings, it's good for you." I hope our children are part of a bigger movement that brings world peace through family peace in the home.

Story: Seeking to Understand Before Being Understood

I would say one of my biggest successes has been stopping

before I react to various situations. One key word that has helped tremendously is being "curious" about our children when they are experiencing their own issues (tantrums, moods, resistance, etc.). Instead of demanding they settle down or go into a time out, I try to stay curious about why they may be having an emotional outburst. This curiosity keeps me much calmer and creates a more peaceful environment all around us. So many times we forget that their little worlds can be shaken by so many things. They don't have the skills and experiences to express their frustration and sadness. It does take a lot of patience and strength on my part. But I have definitely seen it pay off.

In addition, using a non-verbal approach has been such a miracle! I have a hotheaded, power-struggle 5-year-old boy. I can't tell you how many times he has become inconsolable whether he was tired, angry or frustrated. One night my husband came in the room after trying to calm our little guy during the infamous nightly ritual of getting his pajamas on and he said, "I give up." I said, "Watch this." I walked into our son's room, started rubbing his back and asked if he needed a hug. I think my husband thought I put a roll of tape over his mouth! Within seconds, our little hothead reduced his tears of rage into barely a whimper. Within a few minutes, the pajamas were on and he was ready to brush teeth. Wow. The power of touch is amazing.

The class has helped me look to the future and realize how important it is that we give our children the gift of how to deal with various life situations. So many of us think our parenting is okay because "that's how our parents did it" and "we turned out okay, so our kids will be okay." Yeah right. It has forced me to look at my own upbringing which in turn clarifies why I parent the way I do. Ultimately I've learned that remaining confident yet calm with my children can only bring more balance into their lives and ultimately peace into our world.

Story: Repeated Yelling

I have discovered through observation that repeated yelling creates more yelling in the household. Most of the time I yell because I am frustrated, but I wasn't always aware of that. I have observed the more I yell out of frustration, the more my kids yell at various times throughout the day over things that are frustrating them. I can see clearly how my yelling is a way of communicating that doesn't help anyone get the job done. I now use the emotional "pause" button to calm myself and initiate a fresh perspective. Once I calm down and determine what is frustrating me, I can then communicate what I feel and want much better. When I communicate what I feel and want in a calm and firm voice to my children they are much more willing to cooperate with me.

Case in point: I was often frustrated when my kids were

not ready to go to school on time. Yelling definitely made the situation worse as the kids got nervous and cried and slooooooowwed down even more. Instead of yelling to tell them what to do, I learned to communicate in a kind and firm voice how important it is for us to watch the clock, as a team, so everyone gets a good start to the day. Shoes on at 6:45, at breakfast table by 7 am, backpacks loaded by 7:15, out the door at 7:20. We're all much happier when we communicate our feelings and wants along with solutions without yelling. And I've noticed when the day starts on a positive note, the rest of the day tends to follow that path.

Story: Creating Cooperation with Ease and Grace

It was my daughter's fifth year-check up and we addressed her "knock knees." Our doctor said that sitting a certain way was not helpful in her physical development. Knowing I did not want to nag her and that she would not want me to say anything in front of her brothers, we came up with a secret song. Whenever she sat that way I would start to sing: "skidamarkadink a dink, skidamerinkadoo, I love you." She would shift positions singing back to me..."I love you." We would then join together singing 'our song.'

To this day I still sing this song when she sits that way and it always brings a smile to both our faces and connects us.

Teaching Point:

Take a moment and listen to how you talk to your children. What would happen if you spoke to your friends in this way? Not likely that your friends would come back to visit if you told them to clean their plates, to take a learning bite of spinach, not to speak with their mouths full, to use their napkin, and to remember to wash their hands after using the bathroom! Listen to your choice of words with your children or better yet, tape record a dinner session.

Story: Talking With Your Child

Nate, my five-year-old son, had a difficult time behaving appropriately in his gymnastics class. He and I had a long talk and practice session when he woke up yesterday. We cuddled and talked and practiced deep breathing, talked about drinking water, and other things that could calm him down if he got angry. He came up with the idea that he would take his baby doll to gymnastics class so he could be with the baby too while he was calming down.

We went to the gym last night. He set the goal of zero time outs and we reviewed the self-calming ideas before going in. He did great! I asked him how he felt about it later and he looked very proud and said he felt good. Thank you so-o-o much. I felt so much better after explaining to him that it was not that he was behaving badly, which was his first comment during our discussion, rather it was just that it was the teacher's need for a little more calm and quiet.

Teaching Point:

Studies have shown that harsh words used by parents toward misbehaving children could be as harmful as spanking the child.

Recent studies carried out at the Danish Centre for Research, by Ericik Sigsgaard and others, point out that the feeling of self-respect is damaged when a child is punished in one way or another. It seems that it is not much healthier to scold your child than it is to spank him or her. When you punish a child you basically give him or her the feeling that he or she is not worth much.

Studies have shown for decades that children who have been spanked are more likely to suffer low self-esteem and other problems later on in life. Now research has been done that shows the effects of verbal beating.

Children at a nursery were observed and interviewed in a period from 1994 to 2002. More than 50 percent said they hated being shouted at and thought the grown-up was still angry with them long afterwards.

Although spanking children may have declined among many parents, yelling and scolding a child is still very prevalent. How revealing it is to read about one boy from the survey who described scolding as when somebody beats you with his voice.

There are so many ways to tell children what needs to be done in a normal tone of voice.

TIPS:

1. When you feel the urge to yell, take a deep breath instead or walk away until you feel calmer; then go back to the problem. This is also great modeling for your kids.

2. Go to www.IndigoVillage.com and find a Joy of Parenting course or other personal growth courses in your city or call 760-633-3754 and we will help locate one near you.

3. Do an encouragement feast today.

4. Have your child come up with a signal for a power struggle you may be experiencing.

5. Stay curious, seek to understand before being understood.

6. Use one word instead of repeated lecturing or reprimands.

7. Have fun!

Myth Seventeen:
All Children Learn in the Same Way.

If your child is struggling in school, it is not because he/she is not smart. It may be that your child has a totally different learning style than the teacher. Most elementary and middle schools lean toward auditory learning. The kids that excel in this are the ones that learn by hearing. These are the "dream students" for most teachers. Then there are the visual learners. These kids do best if the teacher is a visual learner. You can usually tell what teachers these are because their walls are visually covered with pictures. The kinesthetic kids learn through movement. These are the kids that learn mainly by moving. They process through movement. For many teachers and parents these kids can be their worst nightmares. That may be one of the reasons we have so many kids on some form of Ritalin in this country.

New Idea:
All Kids are Smart, They Just Learn in Different Ways.

Walton Story by Susie

Three of my sons were lucky enough to have Mr. Walker as their sixth grade teacher. Since he was kinesthetic, he had his classroom set up kinesthetically. He also knew how to connect with students and he knew how to make learning fun. My boys thrived in his class.

Teaching Point:

If you want to know more about the three learning styles, I suggest you read *How Your Child Is Smart*, by Dawna Markova. Also, when it comes to schools and teachers, be your child's advocate. It will not do any good to go in and just complain.

Here are some tips:

1. Educate yourself by reading Dawna's book.
2. Volunteer to work in your child's classroom.
3. Make yourself available for field trips.
4. Give your kids the gift of internal motivation so they learn to do things in school because they know they need to, not because they are going to get a reward for doing it.
5. Also watch what you are feeding your kids. That plays a big part in how they focus in the classroom. Many kids today are sensitive to corn syrup, food coloring, and genetically engineered foods. Often those foods will bring on the same symptoms of ADD/ADHD, but when taken out of the child's diet there is a remarkable improvement in their behavior.
6. Supplements are important too. The soil today lacks a large amount of trace minerals. You can go to a natural food store and get colloidal trace minerals. Another fantastic supplement for kids is Blue-Green Algae from Klamath Falls. You can get this easy to

swallow supplement by going to www.celltech.com. Organic food is very important for children of today. You may be thinking that it is a bit on the expensive side, but remember, these are your children. There is real value in providing a nutritious, healthy diet for them.

Walton Story by Susie

Let's spend a few minutes talking about different learning styles. We've got the auditory, visual and kinesthetic learners. My niece, Katie, is very kinesthetic. She loves to move, she learns best while she is moving. She's an incredible athlete. She does best in the classroom when she can be moving around and listening at the same time. Now obviously a teacher isn't going to let 20 kids walk around the room.

I asked Katie, what she has done lately to help her stay focused and move at the same time? She answered, "You have given me some blue green algae to help me concentrate better but I'm still getting there. I think it is helpful to have some things that help me concentrate and move at the same time. When my teachers are reading or talking, I usually keep a ring and a bracelet in my desk and I just fiddle with them. Maybe I could bring some silly putty to class and just play with that in my hands. These things keep me busy while I'm learning."

Teaching Point:

So that's the kinesthetic kids. They can be running all over the house or park when you are talking to them and you're saying, "Are you listening to me?" And they say, "yes." And you say, "How could you be listening if you were moving, tell me what I said." And they can almost say verbatim what you told them. Why? Because they were moving around. Moving is key for these kinesthetic kids.

Now the auditory children, those are the ones that excel in the elementary classroom because they can sit still and listen. They learn by hearing. They don't want to be moving, they want to be sitting and focused and listening.

The visual learners learn basically by seeing. When they see something, they've got it. I'm a visual learner. Once I see something I'm pretty much set and remember it.

We can learn all three ways but we all have our strong way. Start recognizing your child's learning modes. For visual children you may want to have them or you write down the things they need to do and have them see it. For auditory children you just need to tell them. And for young kinesthetic children, I would actually take pictures of them doing what you want them to do so they can see themselves doing it.

In addition to different learning styles in children, there

are also distinctive personality types. There is a group of children today who are especially compassionate and highly sensitive. They have an amazing amount of energy and become easily bored, which resembles a short attention span. Their speech may also seem to be delayed. They resist authoritarian discipline through power struggles and work best within the framework of democratic parenting. These children are often labeled as ADD/ADHD, Obstinate, Challenging, Indigo, Strong-Willed, or Autistic.

What does this all mean? It means that parents and teachers need to start looking at these children from a different perspective. These kids need two main ingredients: to be treated with truth and respect. Let them know the whole picture and they will be more than willing to cooperate with you. From birth up to about age seven they need to be closely connected with an adult. This connection at times can be challenging for a parent, however the connection doesn't necessarily need to be mom or dad, but someone they feel emotionally close to.

When young, these children can have a deep fear of the dark or wake up with nightmares, or just have trouble sleeping. Loss of sleep causes a depletion of serotonin, which in turn can cause hypersensitivity or depression in a child, thus causing decreased focus and low self-esteem. The conflict here is that they need their sleep. What you can do is to be sure they have a "quiet time" every day. This is as important as a karate class or play date. Even after they are finished with naps, a "quiet time" is imperative.

To increase serotonin, your child needs:
1. Sunshine (perhaps building sand castles at the beach or in their sand box).
2. Cardiovascular exercise every day (at least 10 minutes, best if done outside in the fresh air).
3. Breath work (deep breathing).
4. Meditation (visualization or yoga for kids).

Some kids need to be exhausted before they fall asleep while others may need downtime in their bed before they become too exhausted and then fall asleep. If bath-time seems to energize them, then save it for the mornings or afternoons. If the computer or television seems to jumpstart them, then it is best to have it off at least two hours before they head to bed.

Keep sugar away from them in the evening and if they are not lactose intolerant a warm cup of organic milk before bed can be very calming. A lava lamp or small fish tank can be relaxing as can a foot rub with some oil mixed with lavender. When it comes to diet, organic food is the best for these children along with trace minerals. Avoid food dyes and high fructose corn syrup.

Some issues facing these children are: feeling different, heightened sensitivity, idealism, asynchrony (uneven development), inability to accept limitations, guilt from the burdens of the world on their shoulders, deep concerns with morality and justice, lack of understanding from others, and unrealistic expectations of others. Emotional characteristics might be perfectionism, emotional integrity, empathy, compassion, moral sensitivity, concern for justice, and greater awareness.

When it comes to discipline, these children want moral guidance, democratic parenting (doing it as a team), modeling of appropriate behavior, RESPECT – you get what you give, and lastly, but most importantly, unconditional love.

Two of my sons who are now in their twenties display many of these personality traits. Personally I can tell you these children are amazing and wonderful. They are teachers and the gifts they bring are everlasting. Enjoy them and be there for them emotionally and you will not be disappointed in the outcome.

TIPS:

1. Observe your child and see what his or her learning style is.
2. Read the ingredients on your child's food and work on switching to more natural and organic foods and snacks.
3. Volunteer in your child's classroom.
4. Read about different learning styles.
5. Have fun.

A Good Parent Never Thinks of Her of Him Self First.

All too often parents think it is important to put their child's needs before their own or the other parent's. They make sure the child has everything they think they need. Meanwhile the parent is overworked and stressed out and not feeling great about the situation. Another problem with doing too much for our kids is they can develop the belief that "the more you do for me the more you love me." When you stop doing they will feel unloved and get very angry and can create a lot of havoc in hopes you will give in. The other belief a child may take on if you are always doing everything for him or her is that you do not think the child is capable, which can erode the child's confidence. You are also not modeling the importance of taking care of yourself.

New Idea: Take Care of Yourself So You Can Take Care of Your Child.

When teaching I often use the analogy of the flight attendant telling parents to put their oxygen mask on first and then to help with the child's mask. What good are you to your child if you are unconscious from lack of oxygen? The same applies to parenting. If you do not take care of yourself, you will not be the best parent you can be. You also will not be modeling to your kids the importance of taking care of themselves.

Some examples would be to listen to your favorite music on the way home from work, take a ten minute walk around the block with or without your children, take a bubble bath, workout before you go home. As you can see, most of these do not take a lot of time but the dividends are huge for you and your family.

Story: Baby Sitting Co-op

I was a Mom in a rural area, on a tight budget, and my husband worked all day, six days a week. Sometimes the day seemed really long with just my son and I. The baby-sitting cooperative was my savior. This was an ingenious idea where eight or so families got together and traded babysitting hours. We kept track of the hours with coupons and since we all knew one another, we felt comfortable leaving our children with each other. When new members wanted to join, they had to be referred by one of the members. Sometimes I did not have an important social engagement but I would just drop my son off and take a long walk or go home and take a long bath or a nap. Those afternoons of taking care of myself really made me a much better mom and wife.

Story: Yoga for Three

I enjoyed attending weekend yoga workshops before my son was born. After his birth though, I was not sure how this could happen again for a very long time. One day a couple of my friends (one had a baby a little older than mine and the other was pregnant) and I were reading about a weekend workshop to be held just three hours away. We decided to take the workshop as a team. One adult would take care of the two little ones each session so that the other two could take the class. With permission from the yoga instructor, we headed off. It was a very fun weekend.

Story: I am Always a Better Parent When I Take Care of Myself

Taking time at the end of the day to unwind and take a bath while my husband gets our 21-month-old ready for bed is amazing. When I am ready, I read him some books while I am happy and relaxed. He can definitely feel it. When I don't get enough sleep I am short with him. Every Thursday I put Julien in daycare from 9:30 to 3:00. This is great towards the end of the week for me and for him. I get to relax and spend time alone just focusing on me and he gets to spend the day with 13 kids. He loves it and it makes me a better parent and wife. I am so excited to pick him up at the end of the day!!

Story: From an Early Childhood Teacher

I have been an Early Childhood Special Education Teacher for 12 years. Over the years it was my job to learn how to manage young children's behaviors effectively, and I was constantly attending workshops and seminars to learn techniques, theories and methods. When I had my own children, however, most of these ideas flew out the window.

The behavior models based on rewards never felt quite right, and the other techniques basically had me making decisions for my kids and taking control of their behaviors.

As a single mom of a four-and-a-half-year old and a two-and-a-half-year old, I often found myself tired, stressed out and frustrated, especially at the end of the day. Normally a relatively calm person, I found myself yelling more and getting angry. It was not how I wanted to run my household, and I desperately needed a paradigm shift. I found it in my parenting class. Not only did it offer great ideas for working through daily problems, it helped me realize that as a parent it was imperative for me to take care of myself, as well as have the children be active participants in behavior issues. Hearing other parents' stories and ideas was also very helpful and supportive.

I had an idea of how I wanted things to be, but found that by letting some of the less important things slide, the stress level went down dramatically. Instead of trying to fix everything and "make" the kids do things, I found myself letting more things go that just weren't important. When I would find myself angry or frustrated, I would tell the kids I needed some self-quieting space and go sit in a chair in my room. They would see me taking deep breaths and quieting myself down. Not only did it make me feel better, it was a good role model for them when they were angry.

Story: My Mom is my Example
By Katie (14-Years-Old)

To take care of herself, my mom takes the time to make some of her favorite foods. She works out by herself. Sometimes I want her to workout because I know she is happier after she works out. My mom used to work full time and sometimes she would come home tired so I would make her some popcorn with cheese on it. I would then make her take a nap and have a comfortable rest of the day. My mom has taught me to take care of myself too. Some of the things I do are play outside with my friends, play soccer, and for exercise sometimes I go running with my mom or swimming.

Note from Susie: Did you read that part about going outside and playing with friends? Wouldn't it be great if parents had that same concept - to go outside to play with friends?

Story: When Enough is Enough

You need to know your limits. We get into trouble when we try to do too much - out driving with the kids and doing errands, going to doctors, then we come home and think we have to make this incredible dinner. The kids are tired and you're tired and those are the moments when we need to call in the family and say, "kids, we need to do something different tonight, I'm too tired. What shall we do?" You know what they're always going to say, "Order pizza," and you're going to say "okay." Or you're going to say, "Kids, get out the bread and peanut butter." If you're buying healthy, no sugar peanut butter, healthy bread, and organic jam, that's not such a bad deal. Throw some carrots on the side and you've got yourself a pretty well-rounded dinner that is easy and non-stressful. Throw everybody in the bath, jump into bed, and read.

Story: It Takes a Village To Raise a Child, So Create a Village

I know a lot of parents bring their kids to playgroups these days and that's important. You don't need to be doing this parenting thing alone. I don't care if you have another parent with you or if you are a single parent, it takes a village.

When the kids were younger, my girlfriends and I would run. On the way out we might have been angry or upset at our husbands or kids or work. We'd all run for an hour, get a good workout, talk about why we were upset, and by the time we were finished we felt a lot calmer and happier. Remember your kids are part of the village too. When Adam was 10 and I was pretty grumpy that day, he told me to go and take a run. Even your kids know when you need support.

TIPS:

1. Do something to take care of yourself three times this week.
2. Create or join a babysitting co-op or a playgroup.
3. Go out on a date with your significant other or a friend.
4. Stop what you are doing right now and go outside and take 10 deep breaths.
5. Go outside and play for 5 minutes!
6. Have your kids support you in taking care of yourself.
7. Ask for HELP when you need it.
8. Have Fun!

Afterword

My sincere hope is that this book has brought you tips, ideas, a renewed sense of faith in your parenting, empowerment, and smiles. From one parent to another, it is important to remember that whether your child is two or 22, take things lightly and do not beat yourself up over little things. Please remember each day to acknowledge yourself on the things you did well versus the things you did not do so well. Have a sense of humor. Do your best to see the world through the eyes of your child. It can be, at times, quite entertaining and very educational.

The gift that each of your children bring to you is the gift of living in the moment. Soon they will be creating lives of their own, so take time to smell the flowers and relish in the love and connection you have with each of them.

Keep an open heart. Trust that you are the expert when raising your kids.

Love and blessings,
Susie

Suggested Reading

For Parents:

Redirecting Children's Behavior by Kathryn Kvols

Last Child in the Woods by Richard Louv

Golden Rules by Wayne Dosick

Indigos: The Quiet Storm by Nancy Tappe

Positive Discipline for Teenagers by Jane Nelsen and Lynn Lott

Journey to Your Soul's Magnificence by Pamela Dunn

It's Time to Look Inside by Pamela Dunn

For Kids:

The Invisible String by Patrice Karst

Unstoppable Me! by Dr. Wayne Dyer with Kristina Tracy

Incredible You! by Dr. Wayne Dyer with Kristina Tracy

Beautiful Oops! by Barney Saltzberg

I Love You the Purplest by Barbara M. Joosse and Mary Whyte

For the Family:

Little Soul in the Sun by Neale Donald Walsh

About The Author

Susie Walton is a pioneer in parent education. For the past 23 years, Susie has been consistently leading seminars, hands-on workshops, full-length parenting classes, instructor trainings, teacher in-services, and one-on-one coaching.

As a recipient of the San Diego Parent Educator of the Year Award, Susie Walton is a leading expert in the field of communication and relationships with an emphasis on family dynamics. Susie continues to work with a number of various corporate entities and organizations to develop and implement practical and positive change for youth and families.

The fifth child out of a family of ten children, Susie Walton was born and raised in Los Angeles, CA. Susie currently enjoys four sons and daughter-in-laws and 8 grandchildren and resides in Cardiff by the Sea, CA.